YOU CAN

Have a CREATIVE classroom

Sue Cowley

The best-selling author of *Getting the Buggers to Behave* and *You Can Create a Calm Classroom*

FOR AGES
4-7

"When individuals find their creative strengths, it can have an enormous impact on self-esteem and achievement"

National Advisory Committee on Creative and Cultural Education

Author
Sue Cowley

Editor
Kathleen McCully

Development Editor
Kate Pedlar

Project Editor
Fabia Lewis

Series Designer
Catherine Perera

Cover Designers
Andrea Lewis/ Anna Oliwa

Cover photography
© Radius/ Punchstock

Design and Illustrations
Q2a Media

Text © Sue Cowley
© 2008 Scholastic Ltd
Designed using Adobe InDesign

Published by Scholastic Ltd
Villiers House
Clarendon Avenue
Leamington Spa
Warwickshire CV32 5PR

www.scholastic.co.uk

Printed by Bell and Bain Ltd.
1 2 3 4 5 6 7 8 9   8 9 0 1 2 3 4 5 6 7

British Library Cataloguing-in-Publication Data
A catalogue record for this book is available from the British Library.

ISBN 978-0439-94534-9

Contents

Contents

Introduction

As teachers, we need to have a wide range of different skills. Not only must we be proficient in the subjects we teach, but we must also be able to manage a class full of children, in order to let learning take place. On top of all this, creativity plays a vital part in helping us inspire and engage our pupils. It also makes teaching and learning far more interesting, both for us and for our children.

From a very young age, the urge to create is apparent within us. If you give a child some scrap paper and some colouring pens, or even just an empty cardboard box, you will soon see the imagination run riot. Where children use their imaginations, and feel a sense that they are creating something new and worthwhile, this helps to engage them with the whole process of learning.

In recent years, the emphasis on teaching skills has left less room than we might wish for creative and imaginative approaches. Since the introduction of the National Curriculum, and the later additions of the Literacy and Numeracy strategies, the tendency has been to keep the different subjects separate. But at last it seems the pendulum is swinging back towards topic-based approaches to learning, allowing for far more cross-curricular work. This in turn has reopened the door to creativity.

Although creativity is most apparent in the 'arts' subjects, such as dance, drama and music, it can also play a key role in delivering all areas of the curriculum. Where children find the concepts in a subject tricky to access, the creative teacher can use imaginative approaches to bring these concepts to life. In many ways, the less the learning feels like 'work', and the more it feels like focused 'play', the more effective our teaching will be.

In this book, you will find lots of ideas for teaching creatively right across the curriculum, at different times of the year, and throughout the whole of the school. The approaches I suggest are both practical and fun. You should find it possible to adapt them to children of different ages, and also to the different topics that you wish to teach.

Above all else, taking creative approaches will help you enjoy your work as a teacher. And when you and the children feel relaxed and are having fun in lessons, then effective learning will follow.

You Can... **Have a creative 'teaching style'**

You act as a role model of creativity for your children, so show your pupils that you are not afraid to be daring, take risks or even, be a little bit crazy. Let them see that creativity can take place anytime, anywhere – even in the way that you teach them.

Thinking points

● There are lots of different elements that come together to create a 'teaching style'. The way that you use your body, your voice, your gestures and mannerisms and your ways of dealing with classroom management issues – all of these and more come together to create your own inimitable 'style'.

● It can feel a bit embarrassing to get creative with your teaching style, especially if you are not used to being experimental.

● This awkward feeling is part and parcel of being creative. You have got to be willing to take risks, and to overcome your fear of what other people might think.

● When something works well, for instance, your teaching style, it can become very comfortable and a bit routine. To be creative, you need to move outside your comfort zone, from time to time.

Tips, ideas and activities

● Consider which elements of your teaching style have become habitual. Are you always quiet and calm, but perhaps a bit flat? Do you have an energetic style, but lose your temper more often than you should? To explore your style you could:
  ● ask an observer to identify some of your stylistic 'habits';
  ● adopt a completely opposite teaching style for a while;
  ● imagine you are another teacher at the school and deliver a lesson as he or she would.

● Teach without speaking for an entire lesson. We spend most of each teaching day using speech to communicate with our children. Without it, you will be forced into more creative approaches. You might:
  ● tell the children what you want by using hand signals;
  ● use your face and body to communicate your wishes;
  ● draw symbolic instructions on the board;
  ● use props to demonstrate the lesson activity;
  ● prime some pupils so that they can help to deliver the lesson, then stand back and let them get on with it.

● Brainstorm for adverbs with your class and write these words on cards. Pick a card at random and teach in that way for ten minutes or even a whole lesson if you can. For example:
  ● crazily
  ● excitedly
  ● quickly
  ● snappily
  ● happily
  ● sadly
  ● shyly.

● Instead of being your usual 'Miss' or 'Sir', take on different characters as a way of spicing things up. You could:
  ● dress up as an explorer to introduce a geography topic;
  ● act like a Victorian school teacher in history;
  ● become Einstein as part of a whole-school science day.

You Can... **Be creative with your voice**

Your voice is as much a part of your teaching personality as the way that you look and behave. Pupils listen to their teacher's voice for a huge part of each school day. The more imaginatively and effectively you speak, the more you will encourage creative responses from your children.

Thinking points

● Think about some famous people's voices, and how they make you feel. Which vocal styles appeal to you? Which voices do you find irritating and why? What is it about some voices that makes them sound particularly trustworthy?

● Most of us have vocal 'tics', phrases that we use repeatedly, often without being aware of it. Aim to become more aware of your own vocal style. Make a tape or video recording of yourself speaking; play it back and pick up on your own vocal mannerisms.

● Keep your ears open around the school, listening out for what other teachers do and, if possible, observing some experienced practitioners. Consider the children's responses to their teacher's vocal use – which strategies could you adopt too?

Tips, ideas and activities

● Practise using a range of vocal styles for some of the routine tasks in your classroom. For instance, when taking the register, you could:
  ● sing it;
  ● rap it;
  ● whisper it;
  ● perform it as an opera;
  ● read it with an accent;
  ● stretch out each name like elastic;
  ● sing the names on a rising scale;
  ● strum a guitar chord with each one.

● Play around with language in your classroom. Speaking a different language will mean you use your voice, and think, in a slightly different way. You might:
  ● learn to say 'good morning' in ten different languages and teach each of the phrases to your children;
  ● ask any second language learners, in your class, to teach their classmates a few key words from their native language;
  ● speak a few sentences backwards, with all the words reversed. Challenge your pupils to figure out what you are doing and saying: *!do to fun but tough is it*;
  ● devise a whole new language with your class. You might like to look at www.kli.org for inspiration.

● Vocal tone has a powerful impact on children's understanding. It is especially useful for those children who have a limited understanding of English. They can 'read' what a person is 'saying' by listening to their tone of voice. This activity demonstrates the importance of tone:
  ● You need two volunteers; one person is 'A', the other 'B'.
  ● 'A' has arrived in a foreign country and does not speak the language. 'B' is a native of the country who only speaks a kind of gobbledegook.
  ● Person 'A' asks for directions, help, etc. (the other pupils can choose). Person B answers in gobbledegook in a monotone voice.
  ● Discuss why the pupils have no idea what 'B' is saying.
  ● Now try again, this time with 'B' using plenty of tone.
  ● Discuss it again – why is it easier to 'understand' this time?

You Can... **Take creative approaches to routine tasks**

There are many routine tasks that teachers perform every day, particularly administrative jobs such as taking the register. Finding some creative ways to approach these tasks will add spice to your day. It will also encourage your pupils to use their imagination, whatever the activity.

Thinking points

● Routine can be a very good thing: it helps give children a feeling of safety and security. It can also encourage them to behave well, by demonstrating exactly what behaviour is required in a range of situations.

● Too much routine and predictability, though, can make life feel stale and rather dull. It can also stifle imaginative thinking.

● If children get too used to a routine way of doing things, it can throw them completely when something unpredictable happens (for instance, if a supply teacher takes the class). Pupils need to learn to cope with unexpected change.

● Creativity is in many ways the opposite of routine. It is about using fresh and innovative approaches – about looking at old things in a new way.

Tips, ideas and activities

● Make a list of all the routine tasks and activities that are done on a daily or weekly basis, in your classroom and with your class. This might include:
  ● taking the register;
  ● handing out and packing away resources;
  ● lining-up and going to assembly;
  ● a routine for going to and coming back from breaks;
  ● drink or snack time.

● Now consider how you might apply some creativity to some or all of these activities, asking the children for their suggestions. For instance, when lining-up and going to assembly, they might:
  ● line-up in different formats – in alphabetical order, in reverse alphabetical order, boy/girl, facing backwards, with hands on heads, on one leg, etc.;
  ● walk to the hall in a variety of ways – in slow motion, as an animal, in a wavy line, in complete silence (not just no talking, but no sound of walking either!).

● Ask your children to be characters for a day, approaching all the routine tasks 'in role'. For instance, they might become:
  ● police officers
  ● robots
  ● kings and queens.

● Teachers often use storytime to finish the day in a calm and relaxing way. A daily story is a very valuable part of a routine; it also offers the perfect activity for some unusual and creative approaches. You could:
  ● get the children to 'voice' the different characters in a story, with volunteers reading out the lines of dialogue as you read the narrative;
  ● sing the story to the class as though it were an opera.
  ● experiment with different accents;
  ● create an atmosphere by darkening the room and using torches to tell a spooky story;
  ● read the final page of the book and then ask the children to tell a partner the rest of the story.

You Can... Teach creatively across the curriculum

It is tempting to feel that creative teaching only really needs to take place when teaching creative arts subjects. As teachers, we obviously need to use our own creativity during art, music, drama, dance and English work. However, it is important to remember that creative teaching should not just be limited to these subjects, but should permeate all subjects. With a bit of imagination, any subject can be taught in a creative way.

Thinking points

● Where subjects use logic and reasoning, for instance, in maths, we can get trapped into always taking a logical and linear approach to teaching them.

● Where tricky abstract concepts are being introduced, try to find a concrete example so that the children actively 'experience' how the concept works. Teaching creatively will help you do this.

● For children who find it hard to engage with school, or who struggle in the core subjects, a creative approach to teaching is really inspirational.

● We all have our own favourite subjects to teach. If you find yourself less excited about teaching certain curriculum areas, aim to be particularly creative in them. That way you will make these lessons fun for yourself and for your children.

● Taking a fictional approach, and using props and costumes, offers a good way of adding imaginative spice to just about any topic.

Tips, ideas and activities

● Take a topic that you might normally teach in a fairly 'dry' and straightforward way, and think of loads of ways to teach it more creatively. Here are some tips for getting your imagination going:
  ● How can I get my pupils actively involved in this?
  ● Do I know of any stories linked to this topic?
  ● Could I use any interesting props or costumes to teach this?
  ● Can the children 'be' someone else while they are working?
  ● Can I 'be' someone else while we are working?
  ● How might I relate this to any real life or topical events?
  ● Is there any way I can add an air of mystery or intrigue to the work?
  ● Are there any opportunities for cross-curricular input?

● For instance, if you were looking at how to compare and order measures, here are some things you could do:
  ● Get the whole class to line themselves up in order of height.
  ● Use the story of 'Jack and the Beanstalk' to inspire some gardening. Get each child to grow a climbing bean and measure these each week, looking at longest, shortest, thinnest, fattest, etc.
  ● Set up a café in your classroom, based on the *Big Cook, Little Cook* show on CBBC. Use menu items such as 'large drink' and 'small drink' to help you explore different measures.
  ● Enter the room dressed in a white coat, carrying a clipboard. Explain to the children that you are a government scientist, and that you need them to carry out top-secret tests to check on school dinner portions. Discuss some creative ways that you might carry out the checks in secret!

You Can... Share your creativity with your children

Being a teacher can and should be a highly creative job (although a million and one uncreative things tend to get in the way). Teachers use their creativity when working with their children; many also spend time involved in creative pursuits outside school for their own pleasure. Showing our pupils that we have an interest in culture and creativity provides them with an excellent role model.

Thinking points

● Do not assume that all your pupils will have had the same access to creative and imaginative experiences as you have. Some children will never have been to an art gallery, a theatre, a concert or a museum.

● The enjoyment of different forms and examples of creativity is a very personal matter. If you show the children examples of art, music, etc., that you enjoy, this should encourage them to voice their own feelings.

● Become a creative magpie, always on the lookout for interesting samples you can bring into class, such as art postcards, theatre programmes, a new CD and so on.

Tips, ideas and activities

● Talk to your class about your own cultural experiences. Share the feelings that creativity evokes in you, whether positive or negative. Be honest – we have all sat through dull plays or listened to music that does nothing for us. Show your children that it is OK to have a negative opinion about creativity.

● Find examples of your own creativity at home, bringing them in to show to your children. It is not about saying that what you have done is particularly good; it is about modelling the creative process for your children. Here are some ideas:

- Hunt out your old school exercise books if you kept them. Read out a story that you wrote to your class, no matter how dreadful you think it is!
- If you are involved in a creative hobby (sewing, pottery, etc.) bring in some samples of your work. Talk to the children about how you made them.
- If your pursuits are on a larger scale (DIY, gardening), take some photos of what you have done and show these to the class.
  - Ask other staff at the school whether they have a creative hobby they are willing to share.

● When the class is involved in a creative task, we often maintain the role of teacher, so that we can monitor the children's work and behaviour. Sit down and join in the activity occasionally, to show your pupils that you enjoy being creative as well.

● Take your children on creative trips. Many theatres offer deals for school groups, and there are lots of high-quality plays staged for younger audiences. These are often based on children's books such as, *The Gruffalo* by Julia Donaldson and Axel Scheffler (Macmillian) and would feed well into learning, back in the classroom.

You Can... **Use imaginative role play to develop creativity**

Young children spend a great deal of time involved in imaginative role play. As they grow older, we become less accepting of their urge to role play, shifting it into drama lessons.

Thinking points

● Imaginative role play is wonderful for developing a range of skills. It helps children imagine what it might be like to be someone else, to experience different settings and situations, and to interact with a range of characters.

● When they pretend to be someone else, pupils tend to take on the attitudes and behaviours of that person. Children will often behave in a more mature way when they are involved in a role play.

● The classroom can be a rather dull place, with little connection to the outside world. Setting it up as 'somewhere else', even if only for a short time, will give your children access to the wonderful 'real world' of the imagination.

Tips, ideas and activities

● Set up your classroom as 'somewhere else'. Teach for a day with all the learning based in and around this imaginative place, with the children role playing various characters. Depending on your topics and pupils' experiences, you might stick to what they already know, or give them access to an entirely new location. For instance:
  ● 'The market town'
  ● 'The doctor's surgery'
  ● 'The café'
  ● 'The beach'
  ● 'The rainforest'
  ● 'The building site'
  ● 'The zoo'.

● Below is an example of how you might set-up and use your imaginative place, for learning. It is based on 'The café'.

● Before the role play, let the children carry out research into the cafés that they know, and then brainstorm their thoughts:
  ● *Where are they located?*
  ● *Who works in and visits them?*
  ● *What equipment, food, etc. is needed?*
  ● *What decisions need to be made, when opening a new café?*

● Begin the day with a whole-class meeting. Assume the role of the new café owner and tell the children that they have been employed to help you. Split them into groups and allocate various tasks:
  ● choosing the café's name and designing the shop front;
  ● planning the internal layout of the café;
  ● devising a menu for the food and writing recipes;
  ● working out the food and equipment costs and prices;
  ● employing and training staff and creating a uniform;
  ● advertising and marketing to find customers.

● Ask the groups to report back to the whole class;

● Set-up the class café and serve sample meals, if possible.

You Can... Take creative approaches to group work

Group work can provide an excellent structure for creative activities. The children work together to create something new that is more than the sum of what the individuals might have done. However, group work must be managed well if it is going to work effectively, and this means that you must plan it carefully.

Thinking points

● In the 'real world', the majority of creative activities are performed by individuals – the novelist, the artist. Although there is sometimes a team at work, for instance, when making a film, there is typically a director or similar figure in charge.

● Genuine collaboration, where each person has an equal impact on the final result, is hard to achieve. Often, it is about individuals bringing different creative skills to the table, with each contribution enhancing the other; for instance, a song-writing duo where one person writes the words and the other the music.

● In school, we want to encourage collaborative group work, because it asks the children to cooperate and learn together. To achieve this, some children must learn how to adapt their normal roles within a peer group situation.

Tips, ideas and activities

● This activity uses the concept of metaphor to underpin thinking about the roles we take on within a group. The children will need to understand how an animal might be used to describe a person. To get started:

○ Show the children several images of different types of animals (tiger, elephant, dog, pig, etc.).

○ Talk about what these animals are like and the qualities they associate with each animal.

○ Ask them to imagine each animal as a person and talk about what that person would be like.

○ Tell the class what kind of animal you would be and why this animal best suits your personality.

○ Ask each child to choose an animal that describes themselves.

○ Play a few rounds of 'Twenty Questions', getting the class to ask questions of a volunteer in order to guess 'their' animal.

○ Now ask the children to tell a partner what their animal is and why they chose it.

○ Finally, talk with the class about how we might choose to play a different animal in certain situations.

● Use the photocopiable sheet on page 56 ('What's my animal?'). Ask the children to think about the qualities that each animal might have, if they were people, and then look at 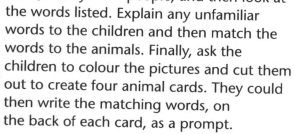 the words listed. Explain any unfamiliar words to the children and then match the words to the animals. Finally, ask the children to colour the pictures and cut them out to create four animal cards. They could then write the matching words, on the back of each card, as a prompt.

● Next time you set a group activity, ask the children to pick one of their animals card at random. Encourage them to take on that role within the group, for example, being 'a quiet mouse' when they might previously have been 'a loud lion'.

You Can... Encourage your children to take risks

We live in a society that is becoming increasingly averse to risk. Children are more and more wrapped in metaphorical cotton wool, protected from any potential hazards. In school, with a rise in litigation and negative press coverage, a 'risk assessment' culture means every possible danger must be analysed and dealt with in advance.

Thinking points

● When we stick to what is safe and already known, there is unlikely to be any genuine creative activity. Without risk-taking, there would have been no Van Gogh, no James Joyce, no Rolling Stones, no Damien Hirst.

● The latest in creativity will often appear weird or just plain silly. Where an artistic creation is far ahead of its time, sometimes a cultural mind shift is needed before it can be appreciated.

● A fear of 'what people will say/think' stifles imaginative and innovative thinking. In a school culture that focuses heavily on testing, it can be hard for children (and teachers) to take risks.

● During any act of creation, an 'internal editor' sits on your shoulder, saying 'don't do that, it's silly' or 'that's not very good'. For this reason, it is best to have a period of unhindered creativity, before editing what has been done.

Tips, ideas and activities

● Hold a 'work and play with someone different' day in your class or perhaps across the whole school. Mix up the groupings that you typically use during lessons. Ask that every child plays with at least one new person during breaks.

● Get your children to do some creative activities, but with a twist. Find a way to deliberately impair their performance, so that they are forced into taking risks, rather than focusing on 'getting it right'. For example, you could get them to:
  ● paint wearing a blindfold;
  ● draw a picture upside down;
  ● write with the 'wrong' hand;
  ● create a sculpture using a knife and fork.

● Take your class into the hall to do some trust exercises. These drama-based activities are great for encouraging risk-taking, because the children have to put their faith in each other. They are also wonderful for developing cooperation. Here are a few ideas.
  ● 'I'm falling!': Working in a small group, on mats, the children stand in a close circle around one volunteer. The volunteer shouts 'I'm falling!' and then 'falls', holding a straight and rigid body position. The others in the group must work together to catch him or her.
  ● Paired obstacle course: Create a simple obstacle course using benches, chairs, tables, whatever you have to hand. The children work in pairs to negotiate the obstacle course – one pupil must keep his or her eyes shut, the other should whisper instructions.
  ● Walking without seeing: You might have to suspend your disbelief to try this one, but it can and does work. Ask the children to stand in a space and close their eyes. When you say 'go', they must walk around the space without being able to see where they are going. They must concentrate hard and listen carefully to avoid bumping into anyone.

You Can... **Help your children to be selective**

A key part of the creative process is the willingness to change, rehash or discard the things which you have made. For every completed work of art or finished novel, there might have been several prior attempts which came to nothing, or which were not deemed 'good enough' for public consumption.

Thinking points

● A willingness to throw away what we have created, without being precious or sentimental, is a critical aspect of being creative.

● At first, your children will probably find this very hard to do. You may also find it hard to throw away work that we tend to think of as 'evidence' of what a pupil has produced.

● Learning how to assess what works well, and also what is not so successful, is a key part of developing creative thinking.

● The pupils need to move away from a frame of mind where they expect to produce a 'finished' piece of work immediately, to one where they understand the process of drafting, revising, editing and sometimes destroying.

Tips, ideas and activities

● Use this sculpture activity to push your children into being selective. Making the decisions as a whole class should take some of the pressure out of the exercise.
  - Give each child a lump of clay or another soft modelling material.
  - Set the children a short time period (about five minutes) to produce a simple sculpture, for instance, of a snake, an apple, a tree, etc.
  - Stop the class and explain to them that they must choose to keep only one sculpture.
  - Give each child a cube, button or other marker.
  - Ask the pupils to walk around and look at all the other sculptures.
  - They should place their marker by the one they think is best.
  - Count up the markers and 'save' one sculpture.
  - Repeat the exercise, aiming to do it several times during the lesson.
  - Towards the end of the lesson, look at the sculptures that were 'saved', discussing how the children made their choice.

● You will need to plan ahead for this exercise, which would work well as an end-of-year activity to encourage selection, reflection and self-assessment.
  - Over the course of the year, collect and keep all drafts and finished pieces of the children's creative work – pictures, stories, poems, photos, etc.
  - Keep these in individual folders or drawers if you have space.
  - At the end of the year, spend at least half a day getting your children to look back over their work.
  - Encourage them to pick out a few drafts and a few finished pieces that they feel have creative potential.
  - Ask each child to present one piece to the class and to talk about why they have selected it. (This does not have to be a polished, end product, but might also be an interesting draft that they would like to take further.)

You Can... Develop your children's creative thinking

Creative thinking is a very valuable skill for your children to develop. It not only helps them in their artistic efforts, but also in their day-to-day dealings with the world. Without creative thought, the next generation of inventions will be impossible. With some very serious issues facing the world, it is increasingly important that our children learn to think creatively.

Thinking points

● The essence of creative thought is to create something new – a new idea, a new design, a new solution to an old problem. Many of the inventions that we take for granted in the modern world (the aeroplane, the car, electricity, the internet), were once the product of someone's creative thought.

● Teachers spend a great deal of time thinking creatively. You might be coming up with new strategies to handle a child with difficult behaviour; you could be devising a new way of teaching an age-old concept.

● The most interesting creative thinking often takes place when we come up against a problem, particularly one that is tricky to solve. The need or desire to overcome the problem forces us into lateral thinking.

Tips, ideas and activities

● A classic creative thinking exercise involves thinking of 'Ten uses for' a common object. Here are some thoughts and suggestions about using this activity:

   ● It works well as a starter, getting the brain warmed-up for creative thinking.
   ● It pushes the pupils into being creative – after using up the obvious suggestions, they are forced into coming up with more bizarre ideas.
   ● Positively encourage crazy, off-the-wall ideas, perhaps by giving a prize for the most inventive.
   ● Where the children quickly get to ten ideas, challenge them to get up to 20.
   ● This activity works well both individually and in groups.

● For the 'Ten uses for' activity, use an object that you can find in great quantities, so that all of the children can actually handle the items. For instance:

   ● a plastic bottle
   ● a piece of string
   ● an empty cardboard box
   ● an elastic band
   ● a paper clip.

● Find storybooks in which the characters demonstrate creative thinking to solve a problem. For example:

   ● *Duck in the Truck* by Jez Alborough (Collins)
   ● *The Gruffalo* by Julia Donaldson and Axel Scheffler (Macmillan)
   ● *The Three Little Pigs* (traditional)
   ● *Cinderella* (traditional)
   ● *The Tiger Who Came to Tea* by Judith Kerr (Collins)

● Ask the children to complete the photocopiable sheet on page 57 ('Creative thinking') for each book. The worksheet asks them to:

   ● think about the problem faced by the book's character;
   ● explain what the character does to solve the problem;
   ● come up with an alternative idea for solving it.

You Can... Offer a range of inspirations

Being creative starts with an initial spark of inspiration, before the longer journey of creation begins. As a teacher, you can provide inspiration for your children, and you can also encourage them to find inspiration for themselves.

Thinking points

● Inspiration is generally a very personal thing, but the youngest children will not yet have a range of experiences to draw on to find inspiration. The teacher can provide them with a starting point, while still encouraging individual creativity.

● Sometimes you might want all your pupils working with the same inspiration – a story title or an interesting image. At other times you could allow them to pick and choose their own inspirational starting point.

● Often, the teacher will be dictating the form of the creativity: *In this art lesson we are going to be doing a painting.* This is an approach borne out of the objective-based way we are encouraged to teach. Consider how well this fits with developing individual creativity: give your children leeway in picking a form whenever you can.

Tips, ideas and activities

● Here are some ideas for finding sources of inspiration to spark your children's creativity (and, indeed, your own):
  ● Sensory responses to a range of materials.
  ● Natural materials from the local and wider environment.
  ● Found objects, both natural and manufactured.
  ● Manufactured objects and materials.
  ● Images from pictures, photos, postcards, paintings.
  ● Sounds – music, but also sound effects and sounds we can make ourselves.
  ● Words – quotes, sayings, phrases, story titles, stories, headlines.
  ● Places – memories of places, imagined places, places seen in a photo.
  ● Problems – how can this be solved?
  ● Questions – the natural curiosity that pushes us to explore.
  ● Puzzles – something hidden, something not quite known or understood.
  ● The imagination – ideas and dreams.
  ● The work of other artists, used as a starting point, perhaps subverting the original style or genre.

● Once you have found a source of inspiration, there are various ways that the children might move on from this starting point. Here are some thoughts as to how you could use and rework Monet's *Waterlilies* painting:
  ● Change the medium: from art to poetry, from art to dance.
  ● Look at it from a different angle: how would the fish see the lilies?
  ● Play around with size and shape: do a close-up on one part of the picture.
  ● Subvert the original style, genre or material: create a pop art version.
  ● Focus on one aspect: use the word 'water' or 'lilies' as a starting point for a sculpture.
  ● Do some detailed research on Monet or *Water Lilies*, and see where it leads you.

You Can... Go on a creative journey with your class

The image of a journey provides a lovely metaphor for the creative process. We start out with a way of travelling (some paints and a canvas, or a pencil and piece of paper) and a destination in mind (a picture of the sea or an adventure story). Sometimes we arrive exactly where we had intended. Often, though, our final destination comes about as an integral part of the creative process.

Thinking points

● The idea of a heroic journey features widely in stories, whether myths and legends or modern day epics such as *Star Wars* and *The Adventures of Indiana Jones.*

● There are some lovely quotes around the idea of the journey that you could use to inspire your children in their creative endeavours. For instance, 'A journey of a thousand miles begins with a single step' (Confucius).

● An effective lesson is often very much like a journey, where the children are on the hunt for knowledge, understanding or skills, and the teacher acts as a guide to help them find these.

Tips, ideas and activities

● Take your children on a journey of discovery, either around the school, in the school grounds or in the local area. Here are some ideas:

  ● Send a group of children with a teaching assistant to 'hunt' for the best display in the school, visiting all the different classrooms. (Ask permission from the other teachers ahead of time.) When they return, they could report on their 'findings' to the rest of the class.

  ● Take the class on a hunt for 'found' objects, for instance, in your nature area. They might collect leaves, flowers, pebbles or feathers. These could be used to create a collage.

  ● Create a treasure hunt in your room or playground. Hide objects in imaginative places (these might be eggs, coins, clues to the treasure). Now get the children to create their own treasure hunts for the class.

● Go on an imaginative journey with your class – this activity is a powerful way of encouraging creative thinking in your children. Many pupils also find it a relaxing and sometimes moving experience.

  ● Get the children to sit or lie down in a relaxed and comfortable position.

  ● Ask them to close their eyes.

  ● Choose a setting for your journey – a forest, a beach, a mountain – anywhere you like!

  ● Talk the children through the journey, giving some detail – but not too much.

  ● Encourage them to use their senses in an imaginative way, for example: *You are in a forest. You look around. What do you see? What kind of trees are in the forest? Can you hear any animal sounds? Now you begin to walk down a path…*

  ● At the end of the exercise, bring the journey to a close and give the children a few moments to open their eyes and 'come-to' in their own time.

You Can... Use the senses to inspire creativity

Our senses can inspire a great deal of creative activity. In return, some creative pieces can bring our sensory imaginations to life. So it is that music designed to appeal to the ear (such as Grieg's, In the Hall of the Mountain King) can make us imagine a craggy, windswept place; similarly a picture designed to appeal to the eye (such as Munch's, The Scream) makes us imagine the sound of desperation.

Thinking points

● Our senses can be a powerful source of creative inspiration. Imagine you have been slogging away at a particularly dull task all morning. Eventually you run out of ideas and your brain feels like it is full of sludge. Simply going out into the fresh air and smelling the flowers will provide an instant uplift to your mind.

● In school, our children tend to use a limited palette of senses – mainly their sight and their hearing, with an element of touch (although not often touch for the sake of texture). Very little use is generally made of our pupils' senses of smell and taste.

Tips, ideas and activities

● Ask your children to keep a sensory diary for a few weeks or even longer. To do this:
  ● Give the children a notebook or a folder, or ask them to bring in one of their own.
  ● Ask them to collect a wide variety of sensory experiences to put in their diaries.
  ● They might stick in a sample (conker, shell, gravel), take a photograph (a stormy sea), draw a picture (my cat), or write a description (the smell of my dad's roast dinner), as appropriate.
  ● Ask the children to decide which senses are most used when responding to each sample.
  ● Get them to draw a hand, ear, eye, nose or mouth (or a combination) to indicate their sensory responses.

● After a few weeks, begin to use the sensory diaries to get creative. You could:
  ● Divide the class into groups and ask the children to share the contents of their sensory diaries with their classmates.
  ● Ask each child to pick one sensory sample from their diaries. Give the class an art form at random (for example, music, sculpture, drama). The children must use their sample as the basis for a creative piece in this art form.
  ● Get each pupil to pick one sample. Set a short time limit of about two minutes. During this time, the pupils must find three other children who have samples that might work well with their own. Once the groups have been decided, the children should choose an art form to work in, producing a piece based on the four samples.

● Take your pupils on a sensory walk or trail around and outside your school. Divide the class into five groups – one for each of the senses. As they walk, the children should collect examples under the headings of see, hear, touch, taste and smell.

You Can... Use deadlines to encourage creativity

Often, the hardest thing about being creative is actually getting started. Putting pen to paper or touching paintbrush on canvas means committing yourself to a definite idea. It can often seem much more appealing to sit around, waiting for a flash of inspiration to hit than to get started. In fact, having a deadline will force you and your children to get on with being creative.

Thinking points

● The deadline might seem to run counter to the act of creativity. Surely we cannot be creative to order? In reality, though, the majority of artists, engineers, writers, designers, architects, etc. do work to a schedule and find it helpful in pushing on with the act of creating something. There is nothing like a deadline to concentrate the mind.

● In the classroom, we work around the deadlines created by lesson length, and by the timetable that our school uses. Chopping lessons up into even smaller chunks is a great way to force your children to get on with it.

● Children can be hampered by the feeling that they must produce a final piece, correct in every way, first time around. Pushing them to work quickly means there is less or no time for them to worry about technique, and their creativity can flow unhindered. They can then use what they produce and develop it into a finished piece.

Tips, ideas and activities

● Plan an art session where the children are pitted against the clock. They must produce a large number of different pieces of work in the lesson, around a single theme. You might like to add an element of competition, to build a sense of urgency: (*Who can create the most different images?*) Alternatively, you could set a short time target for each different task. Set up a still life in the centre of the room and then ask the pupils to:
  ● draw a rough pencil sketch;
  ● draw it from several different angles;
  ● draw it in chalk;
  ● do a painting;
  ● make a sculpture;
  ● create a collage;
  ● take a photo;
  ● do a close-up drawing of one section.

● Look at the main creative task of your lesson and break it down into small pieces, giving each task a deadline. For instance, if you wanted the children to write a poem about the weather they could be given:
  ● one minute to brainstorm all the words they connect with weather;
  ● two minutes to go around the class and gather additional words from other pupils;
  ● one minute to choose their five favourite words, writing these on individual slips of paper;
  ● 30 seconds to arrange these five words into an interesting 'word picture';
  ● two minutes to pick a partner and combine their ten words to create another interesting 'word picture';
  ● three minutes to add alliteration, for example, if one of their words was 'windy', they might add 'wet' and 'wild'.

● On a personal note, if you have always harboured an urge to write a novel, but have never got around to it, you might like to look at www.nanowrimo.org. You could 'win' 'National Novel Writing Month' by writing a 50,000-word novel, in 30 days. A deadline is an effective way to overcome writer's block!

You Can... Use circle activities to enhance creativity

The circle is a wonderful format for stimulating imaginative thinking. The whole class works together, with everyone listening to and building on everyone else's ideas. Where the teacher sets up effective systems, and uses the circle in a bold and imaginative way, this structure can be one of the most creative of all group teaching methods.

Thinking points

● As well as using circles where you stand in an open space with your pupils, consider whether you can set up the desks in a circle or U shape for certain whole-class activities. This format is particularly useful for debates and discussions.

● The circle provides a great metaphor for a collaborative way of working. In the circle, everyone is equal, and everyone's ideas have equal validity.

● Spend time with your children in order to set up your required ways of working, when in a circle. Insist on good behaviour – listening to others, taking turns, being supportive, and so on.

Tips, ideas and activities

● Use the circle format in a creative way. It is easy to get stuck in certain habits (not necessarily bad ones, just routines that can stifle creative thought). Make sure that you vary:
  ◦ the direction you go around the circle. Instinctively, we go clockwise – make sure you go anticlockwise as well.
  ◦ the positions where the children stand in the circle. The pupils will naturally stand in 'their' places. This is easily changed to a more random mix, with a game of 'Fruit Salad';
  ◦ where you start in the circle – if you normally start with the child to your immediate left or right, sometimes ask the child directly opposite you to begin;
  ◦ where you stand in the circle – change your own position regularly, to keep everyone on their toes;
  ◦ what you use the circle for – circle time does not have to mean each child making an individual contribution. You can also do activities where the pupils contribute in a random way.

● Try this drama exercise to encourage quick, creative thinking in your pupils:
  ◦ Place an item in the middle of the circle, for instance, a chair, a box or a hat.
  ◦ Explain to the children that this is a competition – you against them.
  ◦ To 'win', they must keep the item in constant use.
  ◦ When you say 'go', a pupil must dash into the centre of the circle, pick up the item and act with it. It can be anything – for instance, the chair could be a car, a throne or a lawn mower.
  ◦ The teacher wins if he or she grabs the item when it is not in use.
  ◦ To be successful, the children must cooperate, making sure there is always someone ready to take their turn.

www.scholastic.co.uk

You Can... **Be creative with your classroom space**

We all know how much our environment can affect our mood and behaviour. Squashed into a cramped space, some people may soon get tetchy and aggressive; given space, light and air, they can work to their best and feel more relaxed and happy. Typically, we are not given a choice about the classroom space in which we work. What we can do, though, is be creative about utilising it.

Thinking points

● Taking a creative approach to your teaching space will require some lateral thinking. Much of the time, schools rely on routines, consistency and tradition. You might need to take a metaphorical sledgehammer to the way that things are 'usually done'.

● If you need some money to improve your classroom environment, do speak to your senior managers. They may see that an improved environment will be beneficial both to you, your children and the school.

● Pick up creative tips from all those DIY and makeover shows. You might get a team of pupils or even parents involved in revamping your classroom. You could approach local businesses such as DIY stores and garden centres to get some discounted or free materials.

Tips, ideas and activities

● Some teachers are lucky enough to have a great classroom that really works for them and their class. Others are not so fortunate and have to work within a cramped or tricky teaching space. If you have got a difficult classroom, think creatively to try and improve matters. You might:

● Make the most of any awkward features. For instance, in a classroom with a pillar right in the middle, you might make a feature of the pillar, creating a class totem pole.

● turn your space completely around. Where a classroom has traditionally been set up in a specific way, it can be hard to visualise it in a different format. Think whether you can rotate the entire set-up by 90 or even 180 degrees.

● Ditch the debris. If space is tight, you will need to be ruthless. It is hard for creative thinking and effective learning to take place in cramped conditions. Chuck out or relocate everything that is not absolutely essential.

● Reconsider seating arrangements. Look at where the children sit, and think about why you have set up the carpet/desks in this way. Is there another, less obvious, solution for seating? Would a U or block shape work better than groups of desks?

● Here is an idea to try right at the start of term, one that would probably work best for the experienced teacher, looking for a change. Sometimes, a full and busy environment can work against our creative impulses. Why not offer your children a *completely* blank canvas at the beginning of the year? Nothing on the walls, no labels on drawers, no signs for different areas and no lists of rules. Involve the pupils in deciding what their classroom should look like, right from the word 'go'.

You Can... **Create an inspirational environment**

There are plenty of things that you can bring into your classroom environment that will add to your children's potential for creativity. These range from the simple (plants, sculptures) to the more complicated (arranging visits from artists).

Thinking points

● Have a think about the kind of environment that inspires you. Do you feel at your most creative in a clean, uncluttered place, or do you prefer to work with lots of stuff around you? Encourage your children to express their own ideas about what makes an inspirational environment.

● Give your children access to great examples of creativity from history. This will help to broaden their experience and increase their range of potential sources for their own creative efforts.

● Think about the physical, as well as the intellectual, effects of environment. Often, it is the small things such as an interesting scent or an unusual texture that can prove truly inspirational.

Tips, ideas and activities

● Bring in resources that will appeal to your children's senses, for instance, flowers, herbs, spices, fairy lights, recordings of bird song and so on. Fill your classroom with lots of potential sources of inspiration.

● Have an area where you display great examples of creativity throughout history, not just from the European heritage but from cultures around the world. You might include:
  - postcards or prints of important works of art;
  - recordings of music and songs;
  - videos of dancers and actors;
  - copies of seminal novels;
  - images of great architecture.

● Arrange a visit from someone involved in one of the creative industries. There are lots of schemes set up to help you do this. You might like to look at:
  - www.literacytrust.org.uk/campaign/authorvisits.html
  - www.contactanauthor.co.uk
  - www.bowesmuseum.org.uk/learning/schools/stages/
  - www.creative-partnerships.com/projects/
  - www.bigartsweek.com
  - www.createtolearn.org.uk

● Once in a while, do something completely unexpected, with or within the environment, to keep your children on their toes. You could:
  - move the position of your desk and chair, so that you teach from somewhere else in the room;
  - turn one of the displays upside-down and see how long it takes the children to notice;
  - bring in a magic rug or an unusual fabric to cover your normal carpet area;
  - push the desks and chairs to the sides of the room, get hold of a few rugs, and spend the day working from the floor;
  - set up a little mystery in your room that the children must solve – pretend to be as puzzled as they are;
  - turn up dressed as a character from a story, expressing surprise at what the children are doing in your home.

You Can... Get creative with your timetable

A typical primary school tends to have a rigid timetable within which there is very little flexibility. Teachers must use set break and lunchtimes, deliver the literacy and numeracy lessons often at a pre-allocated time, and turn up with their classes for assembly, when required. This rigidity can work against creativity, forcing the teacher and pupils into ever-tighter boxes.

Thinking points

● Some of the ideas suggested here will need the support of a forward thinking senior management team. If you do not have innovative managers, you might try some of the ideas on a small scale. Alternatively, convince them it is a worthwhile experiment by doing an action research project (see www.teacherresearch.net).

● Think about your children's body clocks – how they respond to different activities at different times of day, and how well they sustain their concentration. Adapt your day or your lessons to take account of their varying levels of focus.

● Although children do welcome routine, there is no harm in the occasional day where changes occur. Our pupils need to learn to adapt to the unexpected, and to respond in a creative and imaginative way.

Tips, ideas and activities

● Aim to set aside at least one afternoon, for pure creativity, once a month. During this time:
  - Give your children as much freedom as possible to choose their own form, resources, ideas.
  - Do not designate this time as a specific art, design, drama, music or dance lesson.
  - Let the children take the lead and see where they go;
  - Accept that, at first, they might find it hard to deal with creative freedom.
  - Accept that you might not end up with 'finished work'.

● Spend ten minutes every morning involved in movement and dance exercises, or in an imaginative journey, such as the one described on page 17. These can both have beneficial effects on children's levels of relaxation and concentration.

● Keep a check on how much teacher-led activity takes place in your classroom.
  - Use a stopwatch to check the amount of time you spend talking to the class over one full day.
  - Spend a full day where you cut your teacher talk by half.
  - Consider the impact on your children – does their learning and behaviour improve or not?

● Think carefully about how you format lessons. You might:
  - have five-minute breaks, during longer periods of concentrated work;
  - get the children moving around the room or outside for some fresh air;
  - set aside some time at the end of active lessons for a calming exercise such as 'Sleeping Lions';
  - after calm, quiet lessons, give the children five minutes to let off steam before you continue;
  - get outside to teach whenever you can.

● With topic-based teaching coming back into fashion, make the most of the added creativity this allows. Use approaches where one subject melds into another.

You Can... Manage resources in a creative way

In the classroom, the quality and accessibility of the resources will be fundamental to the level of creativity your children can achieve. Where there is a wide-range of different resources, which the pupils can easily and readily use, the creative options will be far-reaching. Similarly, where resources are limited, the creative responses will inevitably be limited as well.

Thinking points

● The teacher is involved in making creative decisions for the children, simply because of the type of resources that he or she offers the class. For instance, if your pupils are making a collage and you provide feathers, sequins, straws and glue, then the finished pictures will inevitably feature these materials.

● Whenever possible, your aim should be to maximise the choice of resources and minimise your own input with regard to decision-making. This will allow the children to follow their own creative impulses. Encourage your pupils to bring in their own resources for specific creative projects.

● Many teachers have a perfectly understandable desire for a very clear structure in the way that their resources are stored. Sometimes, though, an overly tidy and structured classroom can discourage the children from the risk-taking required for creativity.

Tips, ideas and activities

● Take a look at the labelling systems you already use for your resources and add some creative spice to them. When labelling drawers, you might typically write a label with the name on the front. However, you could also:
- add a picture or photo;
- write the word in a second language;
- stick an example of what is inside (for example, a feather, a cube) on the drawer front;
- stick the labels on upside down.

● Think about the way you sort and classify at least some of your resources, for instance, your art materials. Consider whether a change might be beneficial for the children's creativity. If you normally sort by type (for example, feathers together, glitter together, paints together), you might instead sort them:
- by colour and shade – for example, pinks, from baby pink to deep rose;
- by texture – for example, all rough materials together;
- by source – for example, all natural materials together, such as feathers, leaves and sand;
- not at all! –Throw a big pile of stuff in the middle of the room and let the children grab what they need. We can become overly focused on having a tidy classroom; sometimes creativity demands chaos and lack of structure.

● Encourage your children to use familiar resources in an unfamiliar way. You might need to take the lead in this, but with practise, it will become part of their creative thinking. For instance, here are some ideas for using a ball of string:
- Drag pieces of string through paint to create a line drawing.
- Wrap string around objects to create sculptures.
- Hang different lengths of string from the ceiling in order to display items.
- Dye some pieces of string to create a collage.
- Hang metal objects from lengths of string to create an instrument.

You Can... **Design and build creative displays**

Displays play a key part in creating an inspirational learning environment in the classroom. Your children spend a substantial part of each week in this space, and so the more creative your displays are, the more the children will be encouraged to mirror creativity themselves.

Thinking points

● We might instinctively place displays at our own head height. Take care to put your displays at the level where your children can see them.

● Go a bit crazy with displays – if something does not work, it can be changed or removed easily. Let your imagination run riot!

● Even though putting up displays may no longer be part of your job, it is still a very creative and, I find, enjoyable activity. Why not use displays as an opportunity for some team work between you, your teaching assistant and your children?

● Do not always think of displays as a finished product. A 'working wall' can be equally effective, where the children display ideas and work in progress, changing them as they delve deeper into the topic.

Tips, ideas and activities

● Be imaginative when choosing the spaces and places that you use for a display. For example, you might:
  ● stick some big words on the ceiling above your carpet area, and get the children to lie down to look at them;
  ● have an upside-down display hanging from the ceiling, for instance, a rainforest or under the sea;
  ● cover a window with paper, and cut out a variety of different 'keyholes' for the children to look through;
  ● laminate some work and stick it onto desks;
  ● 'hide' some miniature displays and get the children to find them (for instance, on the underside of chairs).

● Consider how you could get some three-dimensional elements into your displays, to add interest. For instance, you could:
  ● attach some cardboard boxes to the wall, with items hidden inside;
  ● create a 'washing line', hanging display work from it with pegs;
  ● alternatively, and perhaps more interestingly, hang real socks from the line and hide something inside each one.
  ● Put up a 'display tent' and send the children inside to interact with the display;
  ● look at some modern art installations for inspiration. See, for example: www.tate.org.uk/modern/exhibitions/past/ or www.haywardgallery.org.uk/.

● Aim to get lots of interactivity into your displays. By encouraging the children to actively 'take part' in what is on the walls, you encourage them to notice and to respond to it. You can do this by:
  ● using Velcro® so pieces can be added and moved around;
  ● having lift-up flaps;
  ● posing questions for the children to answer;
  ● making displays a multi-sensory experience;
  ● letting the pupils add to the display, for instance, with sticky notes;
  ● having a display table with objects that can be handled;
  ● using some hidden symbols and encouraging the children to find them.

You Can... **Encourage creativity among staff**

Creativity among the school staff might take place on a small scale, just with yourself and your teaching assistant. Alternatively, with the support of the leadership team, it could be done on a school-wide basis. Bear in mind that encouraging creativity needs an element of risk – the need to be experimental and imaginative does not always sit well with strict adherence to schemes of work.

Thinking points

● In schools, tradition can play a key role in deciding how things are done. 'Because we have always done it that way' becomes the reason for a lack of innovation. With the passing of time, and with new children and staff entering the school, the 'old ways' may no longer be appropriate.

● Teaching styles seem to go in circles. For a long time, topic work, with all its creative potential, was viewed unfavourably by the educational establishment. Now, it is back in fashion once again.

● We need to stand up for what we believe, refusing to follow external opinions if we know that they will not work in our classrooms and with our pupils.

● Some of the ideas below will need the support, or at least the approval, of senior managers at your school. Headteachers often like staff to show a bit of initiative, so why not put forward a creative idea and see if you can get the go-ahead for it?

Tips, ideas and activities

● Play around with, and subvert, the normal routines and traditions of your school. Here are some ideas:

  ● Change one of the traditions of your school, for instance, asking the children to help you update the school motto or reinvigorate the school uniform.

  ● Choose one thing and try doing it in the opposite way to that which you have always used in the past. For instance, if you always stage a traditional nativity play, this year try performing a modern version or staging a performance at another time of year instead, such as Easter or the end of the year. Be prepared for some parental disquiet, but be brave!

  ● Arrange a room swap with another teacher (if possible, involve all the staff in your experiment). Spend at least one lesson, and possibly a full day, teaching your children in a different classroom.

  ● Organise a class swap for a lesson, so that you get the experience of teaching at the 'other end' of the school age range.

  ● Put a couple of classes together in a large space, and do some team-teaching with another member of staff. This can work particularly well for topic-based lessons, where teachers are specialists in different subject areas (for example, history and science).

  ● With their permission, swap around the teaching assistants for a day. It can be very useful for TAs to see what the children, within other age ranges or key stages, are doing. They can also learn a lot from seeing how different teachers work.

  ● If you always have teacher-led storytime at the end of the day, then do something different with it. For instance, you could read the class a news story specially written for children (see www.thenewspaper.org.uk) or get pupil volunteers to read some simple books to their classmates.

You Can... Use meeting time in a creative way

In schools, meeting time is often spent looking for solutions – how can we implement these curriculum changes, how should we allocate our resources? There is often not much time or space to spare for anything seen as non-essential. This can mean that creative thinking time for staff often gets shunted to the back of the queue.

<table>
<tr>
<td>

Thinking points

● As adults, we often feel that we must approach tasks in a grown-up and logical way. We put aside the creative, engaging methods we use with our children, and make life unnecessarily dull for ourselves.

● A particular hang-up for adults can be the worry: 'what will other people think of this idea?' Our fear that others might reject, disapprove of or even laugh at our suggestions can be a powerful block to potential creativity.

● As teachers we are used to making presentations to the children, but sometimes not so confident about doing the same in front of our own peer group. This can lead to staff staying quiet rather than putting themselves forward and risking embarrassment.

</td>
</tr>
</table>

Tips, ideas and activities

● Take the pressure off staff, by finding methods which allow everyone to make creative contributions. For instance:
  ● Ask them to post ideas in a suggestions box, to be looked at anonymously after the event.
  ● Suggest that staff divide up for small group discussions, with one volunteer reporting back for their group.
  ● Ask staff to work in pairs, brainstorming ten or more ideas for about three minutes. They should then choose what they feel are their two best ideas. Selected ideas should then be put into a hat. Get a volunteer to pick out one idea for the staff to discuss.
  ● Ask for contributions from staff, before the meeting, creating a 'whole-staff brainstorm' for everyone to explore.

● Here is a fun exercise for encouraging staff to overcome barriers, concerning things that obstruct their personal development, or obstacles to whole school improvement:
  ● Get hold of a range of different-sized cardboard boxes, wrapping them in different coloured paper.
  ● During the meeting, ask the staff to brainstorm barriers, either personal or whole-school (for instance, what they feel prevents the children's behaviour from improving). This could be done individually, or in small groups.
  ● They should then write these barriers on paper, sticking the paper onto different sized boxes, to represent the size of the obstacle to be overcome.
  ● Ask the staff to bring their boxes into a large open area – perhaps the hall or playground, depending on the weather.
  ● Get them to identify either (a) one barrier that might be fairly easy to overcome, or (b) what they perceive as the biggest obstacle to progress.
  ● Now tell everyone to smash up their boxes, starting with the biggest obstacle and eventually pulverising the lot!
  ● Afterwards, talk about how this felt and how they might translate that feeling into action.

You Can... Devise creative assemblies

Assembly is typically the only time during the day that the whole school gets together to learn and celebrate in a collective way. This means it is an opportunity for imaginative activity that really should not be wasted. There are many possibilities for making assembly time more creative, using some very simple yet effective strategies.

Thinking points

● Because they often involve fairly large numbers of children, assemblies do tend to lack interactivity. The format might involve the reading of a story, perhaps with a few questions or points for reflection at the end.

● If we are honest, some children do switch off in assemblies. By adding imaginative, engaging elements to the presentation, this will help the pupils to maintain their focus.

● Many children find it very difficult to make sense of an adult who is talking for an extended period of time. This is sometimes what we ask our pupils to do in their assemblies, for some reason forgetting all the approaches that we use in the classroom!

Tips, ideas and activities

● There is no need to start from scratch when trying to deliver more creative assemblies. Take the ideas and resources you already have, and simply add a bit of spice to your presentation or incorporate some imaginative activities for the children to do. Here are some suggestions:

○ View assembly as a performance, using props, costumes, lights, pictures, music, etc. to grab the children's attention.

○ Make a grand entrance, for instance, whizzing onto stage on a skateboard, for an assembly about safety.

○ Do not always talk from the same spot – force your children to switch their perspective by speaking from the back or side of the room, or by raising yourself up on a desk.

○ Be brave – invite responses and suggestions from the audience, accepting that this might mean you have to think on your feet.

○ Create a visual backup to use any time you need to talk for more than a few minutes. This might mean holding up a prop, having a group of children mime a story, or flicking through some pictures on a screen.

○ Use your voice in an interesting, expressive way, adding plenty of tone, just as you would in the classroom.

○ Whenever possible, get the children to create and present assemblies. Aim for some involvement from different year groups, to get the children to be creative with their older or younger peers.

○ If you have a reasonably small audience, consider getting everyone involved in a collective act of creativity during the assembly. For instance, get a roll of plain paper or wallpaper and roll it out down the centre of the hall. Get the pupils to create a picture together based on the story you have told.

● See the brilliant website, www.assemblies.org.uk for loads of ideas, information and resources.

You Can... Encourage creativity in your outdoor spaces

All schools have at least some outdoor space, whether a tiny tarmacked yard or a large and well-maintained playground. These outdoor areas are a great resource for encouraging creativity and boosting learning throughout the school, both for staff and for children.

Thinking points

- Getting outside for some fresh air can be a great way of boosting your mood when your creativity feels blocked. Simply doing some deep breathing, or some gentle exercise, will increase oxygen levels and aid concentration.

- Giving pupils a specific focus for breaktimes can help minimise disruption, difficult behaviour and the potential for injury in the playground. Where an outdoor space encourages the children to play imaginatively, this will keep them busy and involved.

- Involving pupils in creating and maintaining a green space will encourage them to use their senses, inspiring creativity and promoting learning in science, PSHE, citizenship and geography.

Tips, ideas and activities

- Create a sense of journey and adventure in your outdoor areas, encouraging the children to follow particular routes around the space. You could use the following ideas for play-times and also for lessons:
  - Set up a nature trail with arrows and signs.
  - Create a sculpture park with a winding path to follow.
  - Organise events such as an Easter Egg hunt.
  - Bury some treasure, putting some cards with clues around the space to help the children find it.

- No matter how small or uninviting your outdoor space is, it should still be possible for you and your pupils to develop a garden area. This might be on a tiny scale with pots and raised beds, or on a grander scale with large beds and borders. Depending on your situation and preferences, you might simply grow flowers or branch out into growing your own vegetables. Learning how to dig, sow, plant, compost and harvest their own flowers and fruit is an amazing and creative experience for children. There are lots of projects aimed at encouraging schools to develop green spaces. For some really useful information, and an excellent contacts list, see the 'Schools Gone Wild' project at: www.dynamicearth.co.uk/ documents/wildlife_gardens_key%20contacts.pdf.

- Think about how your playground could encourage more creative play. For inspiration, you might like to look at companies which offer school play equipment. Even if you do not currently have funds available, there are lots of ideas which can be achieved on a smaller scale (such as creating markings for the children to use, on the playground floor). Companies include:
  - www.fawns.co.uk
  - www.creativeplayuk.com
  - www.sportingplaygrounds.co.uk

You Can... Develop whole-school creative experiences

Infant and primary schools vary hugely in size and make-up: from the tiny, rural village school with 50 or so children, to the large, inner-city school with several hundred. Creative experiences can help us connect children of different ages, building a sense of 'family' within a school of any size.

Thinking points

● It is typically rare for the children to be involved in an experience as a whole school. Even assemblies, at which the pupils meet regularly, are not usually about doing something together as a group.

● Where the youngest children are in regular contact with their older peers, and vice versa, this can help build a sense of empathy and collective responsibility.

● Coming together to host a special event can have a real 'feel good' effect on everyone at a school, creating a long-lasting buzz of success.

Tips, ideas and activities

● Celebrate creativity with lots of whole-school events. Involve children from all year groups in:
  ● deciding on the format and contents of the event;
  ● contributing creative pieces for display or performance;
  ● publicising the event to parents and other interested parties;
  ● hosting the event, for example, setting-up exhibits or scenery, showing visitors around, making refreshments.

● Your whole-school event might be:
  ● an art exhibition;
  ● a dance evening;
  ● an evening of music and song;
  ● a series of short plays, performed by different classes.

● Create a collaborative piece of artwork for the school, letting all the children play a part in its creation. For example, this could be:
  ● a mosaic for the reception area;
  ● a patchwork quilt;
  ● a mural for the playground.

● Look into the idea of holding a whole-school thinking day – a day in which all the children are involved in a thinking skills project. This offers a great way to develop creative thinking among and between the different age groups. You might like to look at www.dialogueworks.co.uk/dw/wr/thinkd.html.

● Explore whether it would be possible to have an artist in residence working at your school for a period of time. Approach your local authority to see whether they have any schemes currently running, or whether they are willing to help you find an artist. Of course you do not necessarily have to use a well-known, established artist. Equally, you could:
  ● Ask art students from a local college or university to come in and work with the children.
  ● Contact parents to see whether anyone works as an artist, illustrator, sculptor, designer, etc. and would come into the school to talk about their work.

You Can... **Develop creativity throughout the year**

You Can... # Get creative with the seasons

The seasons can prove very inspirational for creative activities. The contrasts that they provide, for instance, between the heat of summer and the cold of winter, offer a great starting point for work in different areas of the arts.

Thinking points

● The seasons offer us a framework for the year, and for the passing of time. For young children, the concept of longer periods of time is tricky to grasp. Looking at change across the seasons can help them begin to understand this idea.

● The festivals and events that fall within each season can also help us map out the course of the year. Many of these events can provide a fantastic inspiration for creative activities.

● Many of us have a favourite season – talk with your pupils about their emotional responses to the different seasons. Which one do they like best/least and why?

Tips, ideas and activities

● This drama activity will get your children thinking about the things we associate with the different seasons.
  ● Brainstorm, as a whole class, the things that are specifically related to a particular season. For instance, baby animals in spring, falling leaves in autumn.
  ● Talk about the events and festivals that also happen in each season, for example Bonfire Night in autumn and Christmas in winter.
  ● Divide the class into groups of about four to six children.
  ● Ask the groups to prepare four freeze-frames, one for each season. They should include details that will help others identify what season it is.
  ● Get each group to freeze in position for one of the seasons. Look at each freeze frame in turn and work out which season is being shown.
  ● Now work together: bang a drum four times. On each bang, the children move into the next freeze – spring, then summer, autumn, winter.
  ● Choose one season and get the class frozen in position. When you say 'go', everyone should unfreeze and move into an improvisation set in that season.

● Create a poem as a class, using seasonal weather to help your children learn about alliteration. You could:
  ● take a season, for example, winter, and brainstorm all the words you can think of that start with 'w';
  ● look particularly for vocabulary associated with weather, for instance, wild, wind, wet, wail;
  ● come up with a line, such as 'Winter wind wails wild in the woods';
  ● repeat for each of the seasons.

● Divide a square of paper into four and then create a collage for each season, using as much texture and as many interesting materials as possible, for instance, dried leaves for autumn and cotton wool for baby lambs in the spring.

You Can... Use the weather to inspire creativity

We all know how much of an impact the weather can have on our children's behaviour, often for the worse. But the weather can also be used as a great topic to inspire some creative activities in your classroom.

Thinking points

● When exploring this topic, it is fascinating to think about our sensory responses to different kinds of weather. Talk with your class about how the weather makes them feel, and how it might impact on their behaviour and learning.

● There is something very magical about the (these days) rare phenomenon of snow. When it does fall, it really is worth seizing the opportunity and using it as a source of inspiration for some creative activities.

● Both hot and cold weather can have an impact on our ability to learn. If you and your children are working in an overly hot classroom, this will have a detrimental effect on everything you do. Try to find plenty of ways to cool down – fans, blinds, open windows, a walk outside for some fresh air.

Tips, ideas and activities

● Use the photocopiable sheet on page 58 ('The weather') to get your children thinking creatively and considering their sensory responses to the weather. This worksheet encourages your pupils to use descriptive language (focusing on interesting adjectives, for younger children) in order to describe different kinds of weather. Brainstorm as a class to find some good examples, before the children do the worksheet. Here are a few suggestions for 'I am the sun':
  ● I am a big, yellow balloon.
  ● I feel warm and cosy.

Older children could also introduce imagery through use of simile and metaphor:
  ● I am a huge, golden ball.
  ● I feel as warm as a woollen jumper.

● Different kinds of weather can also make us behave in different ways. Try this drama activity, based on the fable by Aesop, 'The Wind and the Sun'.
  ● Read the story to the class (see www.mcwdn.org/fables/windsun.html).
  ● Talk about the moral of this fable.
  ● Discuss what kind of characters the sun and wind are.
  ● Divide the class into groups of three.
    ● One child plays the sun, one the wind, the other a traveller. If possible, give each traveller a piece of material to act as a cloak. (Alternatively they might just use their coats.)
    ● The children then re-enact the story.
    ● The children playing the sun and wind must take it in turns to act as the types of weather; the other child must be persuaded to respond.
    ● Give the children a set of contrasting kinds of weather, for instance: sun and rain, sun and wind, rain and snow.
    ● For brief outlines of many of Aesop's other fables, see also www.businessballs.com/aesopsfables.htm.

You Can... Get creative at Christmas time

Christmas is often a time in schools when there is plenty of creativity taking place. As children and teachers wind down towards the holidays, there seems to be more space for art, craft and other creative activities, within the busy school day. This in turn creates a real buzz of excitement in the classroom.

Thinking points

● Tradition plays a key part in the way that we celebrate Christmas – from the Christmas tree to the Christmas pudding, there is a long history associated with the season.

● Sometimes, though, tradition can mean we forget to try something new, repeating the patterns of the past rather than being genuinely creative. By trying some new or original activities with your class, you can help them create their own traditions for the future.

● There are plenty of suggestions for creative Christmas activities on the internet – try doing a web search to find loads of new ideas.

Tips, ideas and activities

● If you normally have a traditional Christmas tree in your classroom or school, try something different for a change. You could:

  ● get hold of a large, bare branch and decorate it sparingly, perhaps in a simple colour theme such as white and silver;

  ● buy a real Christmas tree in a pot – bring it into your classroom as festivities develop, then return it outside so it can be reused next year;

  ● make 'tiny trees' for each child to take home – use an empty yoghurt pot as the base, and a pine cone as the tree, decorating it with paint, glitter, sequins, etc.

● Christmas can be a time when lots of waste is generated. Try an environmentally-friendly theme for Christmas in your classroom. For instance, you could:

  ● look at examples of the packaging used for toys, food, etc. and talk with the children about how to avoid using it;

  ● get the children to create some home-made wrapping paper;

  ● encourage your pupils to create, rather than buy, gifts for their families, for example, by offering a service (car washing, gardening) as a present;

  ● collect Christmas cards over the holiday season and either (a) reuse these in the classroom, for instance, punching holes in them and using them as cards for weaving, or (b) recycle them, perhaps through a supermarket scheme;

  ● help your pupils create a Christmas e-mail or send an e-card.

● Take a creative approach to your Christmas show, using a modern Christmas story to inspire you. For instance:

  ● *Little Miss Christmas* by Roger Hargreaves (Egmont Books).

  ● *The Best Christmas Present in the World* by Michael Morpurgo (Egmont Books).

  ● *The Jolly Christmas Postman* by Janet and Allan Ahlberg (Viking Children's Books).

You Can... Use birthdays as a theme for creativity

Our birthdays mark the passing of another year, and for young children each birthday can seem a very long time coming. When a birthday does arrive, though, it is a time of great excitement, enjoyment and celebration.

Thinking points

- Increasingly in our culture, children's birthdays have become a time for excessive spending and consumption. You might like to get your children thinking about creative ways to have fun or make gifts *without* needing to spend money.

- Consider marking each pupil's birthday in a creative way, for instance, with some singing or by letting the class choose a few imaginative games to play.

- Organising a birthday party can be a very creative activity – you might like to adapt the birthday cake idea by asking your pupils to arrange a party for a favourite character.

Tips, ideas and activities

- Ask your children to tell or write a story called 'The best birthday present in the world'. Encourage them to think laterally and creatively about what the best present would be – it might not be something that can be bought at a shop.

- Use a range of stories, fairy tales and nursery rhymes to get your children thinking about what different characters might want for their birthdays, and why. For instance:
  - Humpty Dumpty might want a big pot of glue to mend himself.
  - Cinderella might want a real golden coach to replace the pumpkin.
  - Little Bo Peep might want a magic sheep-finding device.

- Use the photocopiable sheet on page 59 ('The birthday cake') to get your children designing an imaginative birthday cake for their favourite character.
  - Brainstorm lots of different characters with your class – include characters from storybooks, fairy tales, television programmes, cartoons, etc.
  - Talk about the kind of cake these characters might want – what sort of ingredients would they like? What kind of decorations would they enjoy?
  - For instance, Fifi from the *Flowertots* would probably like her ingredients to include vegetables and edible flowers and a garden theme to the decorations.
  - The worksheet includes a wordbank – go through these words with the class and perhaps make a longer list on your whiteboard.
  - Once they have chosen a character, the pupils draw the decorated cake on their worksheet, if possible adding collage effects such as sequins and glitter.
  - They should then write out some instructions for decorating the cake.
  - If there is time, the children could make a three-dimensional model of their cake.

You Can... **Encourage creativity during the holidays**

For those children whose parents are able to take them to exotic or exciting destinations, the holidays offer a wonderful opportunity to experience other cultures and places. For some children, though, a break from school means little more than a long period of boredom.

Thinking points

● By using their imagination, even those children with a lack of opportunity to travel and go out on day trips can still 'experience' what it might be like to visit somewhere different.

● When thinking about this topic, try to ensure that you still include those children who are unlikely to travel to exotic destinations.

● With so much class time spent on literacy and numeracy, it is increasingly vital that children have the space to be creative outside of school.

● As you might remember from when you were young, the long summer break can seem endless. Encouraging your children to do something creative during the holidays will help them focus their energies.

Tips, ideas and activities

● Carry out some tasks based around the idea of creative packing. The children could:
  ● suggest five items they would want to have if they were stranded on a desert island;
  ● work in groups to see how many blocks they can pack in a box;
  ● plan their packing for a trip to somewhere very hot or cold;
  ● pack a bag for a story character, for instance, for Cinderella's honeymoon.

● 'I'm bored!' is a familiar complaint to many parents, particularly during the long summer break. Get your class to brainstorm creative ways of overcoming boredom. For example, they could:
  ● offer to help out with tasks around the home, such as hoovering or cooking;
  ● ask their parents or guardians to organise a picnic in the back garden;
  ● do some art-based activities, such as junk-modelling, sticking or colouring;
  ● ask for a pot in which to grow a plant;
  ● set up a farm or obstacle course in the garden.

● Challenge the children to do at least one of these things over the break, reporting back on what they did.

● Write postcards as if they were being sent from exotic or 'out of this world' destinations. What would someone write if they were on holiday:
  ● on a distant planet?
  ● on a submarine deep in the ocean?
  ● a hundred years ago?

● Ask the children to collect unusual items, during the break, for a 'Show and Tell', when they return to school. For instance:
  ● a handful of sand from a beach that they visited;
  ● a menu or napkin from a restaurant where they ate;
  ● a bus or train ticket;
  ● a ticket from a trip to the theatre or cinema.

You Can... Use props to inspire the imagination

Drama is, of course, wonderfully creative. By pretending to be someone else, in a different time, place or situation, your children can experience worlds far removed from their own. Giving your pupils an object to use as a 'prop' will help them engage with the drama activities and encourage them to use their imaginations.

Thinking points

● Using props is a great way to get your children thinking creatively. To find a prop, simply look around at school or at home, to find an object that could be used in a range of different ways.

● The simpler the prop, the more your pupils will have to use their imagination and their acting skills in order to turn it into something else. Something as straightforward as a stick, a balloon or a cardboard box can be transformed into a whole range of other items.

● By imagining that an object is 'something else', your children will begin to understand the high-level concept that one thing can symbolise or 'stand for' another.

Tips, ideas and activities

● Stand the class in a circle. Put an empty box in the middle. Now challenge the children to 'use' the box in a range of ways. Their aim is to stop the teacher from 'winning' the box. The teacher 'wins' by getting to the box when it is not being used. Among many other things, the children might use the box as:
  ● a shoe
  ● a hat
  ● a car
  ● a sink
  ● a football.

● Pass the box around the circle, asking your children to imagine that various different things are inside it. They should pass it in a way that shows exactly what is inside. For example:
  ● an incredibly fragile glass ornament;
  ● a wild and dangerous animal;
  ● a bomb that could explode if it is not kept really still;
  ● a heavy weight that the children can hardly lift.

● Now pass some 'invisible' items around the circle. Again, ask the children to show what the item is by the way that they handle it. You might decide to tell the pupils what the item is, or ask them to guess by the way that you handle it. Your objects might include:
  ● a wriggling snake that wants to escape;
  ● a balloon that threatens to float away;
  ● a burning hot piece of metal.

● Divide the class into pairs and give each pair a simple object, such as a balloon or a large sheet of paper. Ask the children to develop an improvised scene in which their object becomes something else. For instance, the sheet of paper might be used as:
  ● a raft
  ● a wall
  ● a stepping stone

You Can... Create a range of interesting sounds

Rather than always using ready-made instruments for music sessions, it can prove far more inspiring if children create sounds through other means. They can use their bodies, objects or natural materials to create a whole host of interesting sounds.

Thinking points

● Our classrooms are typically filled with the fairly monotonous sound of teachers and children talking. Finding more creative ways to make noise can provide a welcome relief from constant chatter.

● Silence can also provide a good contrast to the constant noise of school. It is also great for reflection, relaxation and sense of calm. Aim to incorporate a period of silent time into each school day.

● Rather than using your voice to get your class to be silent, try using some unusual percussive sounds or noises instead. Because they are unusual, these are far more likely to get the children's attention.

Tips, ideas and activities

● Make instruments using various resources. For instance:
  ● empty plastic bottles;
  ● beans, shells and gravel;
  ● paperclips and other metal objects;
  ● hollow bamboo canes of varying thickness;
  ● sticky items, such as sticky tape and sticky labels;
  ● thin sheets of Perspex.

● Explore the noises which can be made using natural materials in an outside space. In groups, the children could:
  ● bang a stone against the ground;
  ● rub a stick against a wall;
  ● tear up dried-out leaves;
  ● swish through long grass.

● Get the children to create a variety of weather sounds, using only their bodies. They might:
  ● drum their fingertips to make the sound of rain;
  ● rub their fingers on the floor to create a wind sound;
  ● stamp their feet to make the sound of a storm;
  ● use their voices to make a whistling wind sound;
  ● click their tongues against the roofs of their mouths for raindrops.

● Split the class into groups to create a storm, using only body sounds. Tape-record the 'storm' to use in a piece of drama.

● Ask your children:
  ● What is silence?
  ● How do we 'make' it?
  ● How do we feel when there is silence?
  ● Can it ever be totally silent?

● As a class, try to be *completely* silent for a few minutes. Afterwards, talk about any sounds the children heard.

● Make different rhythms, for example, by:
  ● tapping pens on desks;
  ● tapping fingers on palms;
  ● humming.

You Can... **Get creative with costumes**

From a very young age, children love to dress up – whether this is kitting out a doll or teddy in a different outfit, or putting on a costume and pretending to be someone else. Wearing an item of someone else's clothing can help your pupils imagine what it might be like to be that person.

Thinking points

● Costumes add a lovely touch of colour and inspiration to the classroom. While it may be felt that school uniform takes away individuality, costumes are all about celebrating it.

● Looking at costumes from around the world can be a great way of introducing the children to different cultures and beliefs.

● Using costume does not have to be difficult – something as simple as a hat or a pair of gloves can inspire lots of imaginative activities.

● Children always love to see their teachers 'mucking in'. If you have the nerve, do put on some costumes yourself. Taking on a different character, in order to introduce some more unusual, drama-related work, can be a great way of engaging your pupils.

Tips, ideas and activities

● Get hold of lots of different accessories, such as hats, shoes, gloves, ties. Explain to the children that these are 'naughty clothes', which will not do what they are told. Ask for volunteers to improvise with them. For instance:
  ● the hat that won't stay on;
  ● the gloves that refuse to come off;
  ● the shoes that walk too fast;
  ● the belt that won't do up.

● Organise a 'fashion show' with your children to spark off lots of creative activity. The pupils could:
  ● design, make or bring in different clothes;
  ● prepare a commentary for the show;
  ● choose music and create special effects;
  ● model their outfits in front of an invited audience.

● Find a range of different pairs of shoes (charity shops can be a cheap place to buy these), and ask your children to 'stand in someone else's shoes'. What kind of person or character would they be if they were wearing:
  ● Wellington boots?
  ● clogs?
  ● cowboy boots?
  ● slippers?
  ● trainers?

● If you are willing, get dressed-up yourself as a character, in order to inspire some imaginative activities. You might:
  ● wear a lab coat and become a government scientist for some science work;
  ● put on a police helmet and get the children to write, in character, as detectives;
  ● get kitted out in Victorian clothing and become a Victorian teacher for some history work.

● Bring in costumes and accessories from around the world, or use pictures. If you work in a multi-cultural school, ask around to see whether parents are willing to lend you an Indian sari, a Maori mask, a Japanese kimono, etc. Talk with the children about why these costumes are beautiful and what they might mean to the people who own them.

You Can... Use shape in a creative way

Shapes are a key feature of maths work for children of this age; your pupils will also be learning the various shapes that go together to form letters during literacy lessons. Shapes also play a key role in the arts subjects, and can lead to some highly creative and imaginative work.

Thinking points

● Using creative approaches to working with and learning about shapes will back up the work you do in areas such as maths and literacy.

● For children who like to learn in a kinaesthetic way, actually making the shapes with their bodies will prove much more memorable and engaging than simply drawing them on the page.

● Many of the shape activities described here will also teach your children how to cooperate with other members of the class. They will also help your pupils develop their focus and concentration.

Tips, ideas and activities

● Use these movement activities to explore different shapes:
  ● Using just your fingers, make a square, circle and triangle.
  ● Now do the same with your hands and then try this using your arms.
  ● Working in a group, make various shapes with your bodies.
  ● As a whole class, switch from a circle shape into a square.

● Use this movement exercise to learn about and work with triangles:
  ● Take the class into an open space.
  ● Ask the children to stand in a space on their own.
  ● They should pick two other children, without saying whom they have chosen.
  ● The pupils now move around the space, in any direction they like.
  ● The aim, for each child, is to create and maintain a triangle shape with the two people they have picked. As they move further apart, the child moves further away, and vice versa.

● This art activity will encourage your children to use circles in a creative way. For each child, you will need:
  ● a picture – a photo, a famous painting or an advert;
  ● two blank sheets of A4 paper: one with a small circular hole cut in it, the other cut into a large circle;
  ● a handful of paperclips;
  ● some pens, paints or other drawing materials.

● To do the activity, the children:
  ● use the circular hole as if it were a viewfinder or microscope;
  ● move it across the picture to explore what they can see through it;
  ● find the most interesting part of the image and clip the paper to it, using paperclips;
  ● draw an enlarged, close-up version of what they can see on the sheet of circular paper;
  ● talk about why they chose this particular part of the image.

You Can... Use movement in a creative way

Children love to move and use their bodies – in fact it is often hard to get them to stay still, which is what a lot of school work requires. Movement activities lend themselves to some wonderfully creative responses, and many can be used as a quick break, during long periods of concentrated work.

Thinking points

● Movement can be used in a creative context across all the arts subjects: in dance, but also in drama, music and art lessons.

● Allowing your children to move around for a little while will often ensure better concentration when they do have to sit down again.

● If you are concerned about your children getting over-excited during movement sessions, make sure that you incorporate a calming down activity at the end. This can be something as simple as a few minutes spent as 'Sleeping Lions' or frozen statues.

Tips, ideas and activities

● Find lots of creative ways to move around an open space. The children could:
  ● walk across something dangerous: a muddy mountain, a snowy wilderness, sinking sand, broken glass;
  ● walk with an emotion: sad, happy, angry or scared;
  ● walk as a character: a police officer, a king or queen, a sumo wrestler;
  ● walk like an animal: slither like a snake, thud like an elephant.

● Now repeat some of these ways of moving, this time adding sounds, noises or speaking while you walk.

● Get your children thinking about moulding and positioning their bodies, using a 'Lump of clay' activity. Here's how it works:
  ● Divide the class into pairs – one pupil is the 'lump of clay', the other pupil is the 'sculptor'.
  ● The sculptor has one minute to mould his or her partner into an unusual or interesting position.
  ● At the end of the time, 'freeze' the class.
  ● Now all the sculptors take a walk around the room, looking at everyone else's clay models.
  ● Repeat the activity with the pupils swapping roles.

● Use contrasts to create interesting movement. Give ten beats on a drum; with each beat, the pupils make a gradual change from one to another, for example, changing from:
  ● up to down;
  ● silent to noisy;
  ● hot to cold;

● To help your children keep their focus, intersperse long periods of concentration with quick movement activities. For example, ask the children to:
  ● take a walk around the room then return to their seats;
  ● stand up, turn in a circle, then sit back down;
  ● 'shake-out' their hands regularly during a period of writing;
  ● do a range of Brain Gym® exercises.

You Can... Create interesting and imaginative characters

The best stories are full of characters that grip the imagination – people, animals or imaginary beings that are both interesting and unusual. These characters push the story forward through the force of their personalities. The reader associates with the characters, and this association keeps us involved with a story.

Thinking points

- When they first write stories, children tend to stick to characters that they already know. This usually involves their immediate circle – themselves, their friends and their family. You might also spot characters taken from stories that your pupils have read.

- It is not easy to develop original characters; even older pupils find this difficult to do. However, you can certainly get your children to start using their imaginations to think about who or what might make for an interesting story.

- Giving your children a visual stimulus for a new character can be a great way to get them started. Similarly, thinking about how specific objects might be linked to a particular person offers a 'hands-on' approach to character development.

Tips, ideas and activities

- Make some mismatched character collages:
  - You will need lots of magazines, some paper and glue.
  - The children cut out a different body part, from photos of various people.
  - They join these together to make one weird character.
  - When these are finished, get the pupils into pairs.
  - Ask them to develop a storyline together, featuring their two oddball characters.
  - Alternatively, they might come up with dialogue that each of the characters would say to each other.

- Build a character as a class, by using the starting point of 'the bag that got left behind'. Here is how it works:
  - Find an interesting looking bag – a suitcase, a rucksack, an 'old lady's' handbag.
  - Fill it with items that might be connected to a character.
  - Be as imaginative as you like – for instance, your suitcase might be filled with bunches of bananas, a leaflet from a zoo and a plane ticket to Africa.
  - As a class, talk about the various items, and what kind of character might have left the bag behind.
  - Develop a story based around this character, either written, or improvised as a drama activity.

- Characters that face an obstacle or problem are always more fascinating. Use the format of 'the *animal* that couldn't...' to develop imaginative characters. For example:
  - the fish that couldn't swim;
  - the snake that couldn't hiss;
  - the bird that couldn't fly.

- Similarly, characters who are '*very*' something will be more vivid and interesting. You might tell the story of:
  - the very ugly princess;
  - the very old giant;
  - the very scared monster.

You Can... Develop creative storylines

When we ask our children to sit down and write a story, they will often come up with something fairly mundane. We need to show them how to make their storylines more interesting, and get them experimenting with different techniques and approaches. This will help our pupils learn to write in a more inventive and creative way.

Thinking points

● Perhaps surprisingly, putting tight constraints on how a story is written will often free-up the writer to show greater creativity. These constraints might be to do with form, structure, character, dialogue, etc.

● Having a sense of their audience, and understanding what that audience needs, wants or expects from their story will really help your children develop their creative writing.

● Sometimes, though, it works better to go against what the audience might be expecting, and to incorporate an unusual element or a surprising event. Subverting audience expectations can lead to some very humorous and interesting outcomes.

Tips, ideas and activities

● Retell a traditional story, getting your children to subvert the original in some way. For instance, they might use an alternative perspective, a different form, or a character that does not do what is expected. Here are some ideas to get you started:
  ● 'Little Red Riding Hood' retold from the viewpoint of the Wolf;
  ● 'Humpty Dumpty' retold as a news report;
  ● 'Cinderella' retold with Cinderella turning the prince's proposal down.

● Use dialogue as a starting point for developing a storyline. Here is how the activity works:
  ● Write a number of different snippets of dialogue on slips of paper.
  ● You might create these snippets yourself, or ask the children to collect examples for homework (for instance: 'Help! I can't hold on much longer!'; 'Whatever you do, don't go in there'; 'Can you believe he would say such a thing?').
  ● Divide the class into small groups.
  ● Give one line to each of the children.
  ● The pupils develop a piece of drama, using all the lines of dialogue.

● Adding some constraints to a story can actually force your children to be more creative. Try the following exercise:
  ● Get the children to write down: a colour, an animal, a place and an object.
  ● So, they might choose: blue, elephant, shop, pencil.
  ● Ask them to write a story that includes their four words.
  ● Alternatively, get the children to fold up their pieces of paper and put them all into a bag.
  ● The pupils now get to do a 'lucky dip' and must write a story using the ideas they draw out.

● Other constraints might include:
  ● writing a story without using the word 'the';
  ● telling a story using only 20 words;
  ● writing a story without using any adjectives.

You Can... Get creative with fantasy worlds

The idea of a fantasy world, one completely removed from our own, is very appealing. Books such as The Lost World by Arthur Conan Doyle and the Discworld series by Terry Pratchett, and films such as Jurassic Park, all offer us a glimpse of imaginative and exciting places.

Thinking points

● This theme is one that will really get your children thinking creatively – their fantasy world might be in a different time, place or dimension, and will certainly include some unusual and imaginative characters.

● From a young age, children are fascinated by imaginary creatures, such as dragons, and also by those that no longer exist. Dinosaurs hold a perennial fascination, and seem to interest and excite children, rather than scaring them, as might be expected.

● The Primary Framework for Literacy uses 'fantasy worlds' as a theme for writing narratives at Key Stage 1. This theme has great potential as a source of inspiration for creative writing.

Tips, ideas and activities

● Show the children some images or photographs of unusual landscapes or places, for instance, a forest in the mist, a volcanic landscape. For each picture, ask the children to imagine:

  ● Stepping into the picture, then turning right and walking forwards – what kind of things do they see?
  ● Using all their senses – what can they smell, hear, taste, touch and see?
  ● Meeting a character (animal, human or other!) – what kind of character is it and what is the character doing?
  ● Seeing a strange building – what kind of building is it (tower, run-down shack) and who lives inside?
  ● Looking down and seeing a magical object at their feet – what is it, who has left it there and what magical powers does it have?

● As a class, brainstorm all the different locations where you might find a fantasy world, and what these environments would be like. Focus your children on their sensory responses. For instance:

  ● an underwater cavern;
  ● a plateau where time has remained 'frozen' (you will probably need to explain what a plateau is);
  ● a familiar place, but back in a time before humans walked the Earth;
  ● a jungle full of strange creatures.

● Use the photocopiable sheet on page 60 ('My fantasy world') to get your pupils brainstorming sensory vocabulary and developing a story. They should:

  ● Write down the location they have chosen.
  ● Make a list of all the words linked to this place, in the columns, using each of the five senses.
  ● Younger children might draw pictures instead.
  ● The pupils then use the boxes at the bottom of the page to draw either (a) a cartoon strip about their fantasy world or (b) a storyboard to help them write a story.

You Can... Inspire your children to write poetry

The best poems use language in a highly creative way, whether this is through unusual images that stimulate our senses, or through making the most of the way that language sounds. Poetry is, of course, the ideal form for reading to your children – it is typically short and often is at its best when read out loud.

Thinking points

● Your children will probably have some preconceptions about poetry, for instance, that it always has to rhyme. It is well worth taking the time to talk about what poetry is and what it can make us feel.

● The more examples of poetry you read to your children, the more they will develop their own personal responses to the form, and the more able they will be to write their own poems.

● Many primary teachers spend a great deal of time reading stories to their classes; and probably a lot less reading the children poetry. Why not spend one half term reading your class poems at storytime instead of books?

Tips, ideas and activities

● Before your children begin to write their own poetry, talk with them about what makes a poem. Read several different poems to the class and then ask:
  - Do poems have to rhyme?
  - What's the difference between poetry and stories?
  - What makes a 'good' poem?
  - What kind of language does a poem use?
  - How do you feel when you listen to poetry?

● Find lots of ways of sparking off the initial inspiration for a poem. You could try using:
  - a bag containing lots of interesting words; pull some out as a starting point;
  - things that encourage sensory responses, such as natural materials and food;
  - a brainstorming session around a single word, such as 'cat'. Consider each of the senses to find interesting vocabulary.

● This selection exercise will show your children how to pick the best words for a poem:
  - Select a theme, for instance, 'In the woods'.
  - Spend ten minutes writing a story around this theme.
  - They should write as much as possible, without worrying about spelling, punctuation, etc.
  - At the end of the ten minutes, they count the number of words and write this at the bottom.
  - They divide this number in half (for example, 40 words = 20).
  - They cut exactly this number of words from the page, crossing out any less interesting words.
  - Repeat the exercise, so that the number is cut in half again (20 words = 10).
  - They then cut this number of words from the page, ending up with a quarter of the original total.
  - They write each of these words on a slip of paper.
  - They can then arrange the words into a poem or word picture.

You Can... Get creative when writing instructions

We all know just how frustrating it can be to try to follow badly written instructions, especially when trying to construct flat-pack furniture! Luckily, the kind of instructions your children will be writing are not quite as complex, but getting them written correctly is still crucial.

Thinking points

● Writing instructions is one of the first types of non-fiction writing that your children will do. Unfortunately, this topic has the potential to be rather 'dry' and dull, in contrast to some of the more engaging areas available for imaginative writing.

● By taking a creative approach to this activity, you will show your children that non-fiction writing can be just as engaging and interesting as narrative.

● The key features of a good set of instructions are that they are easy to read and follow, that they are given in the correct order, and if possible that they have some kind of visual aid to understanding.

Tips, ideas and activities

● As a starter activity on this topic, ask the children to direct a partner through an obstacle course using a series of instructions, such as 'take three steps forward', 'turn right'. Discuss what makes a 'good' set of instructions.

● Use this 'hands-on' activity to get your children engaged with the idea of giving instructions. Here is how it works:
   ● Divide the class into groups of four.
   ● Give the groups the equipment and ingredients needed to make a simple food, for instance, a jam sandwich or an iced and decorated fairy cake.
   ● They will also need four small blank cards per group.
   ● Ask the children to discuss the instructions that are needed to make the food, coming up with four steps that they must take, in the correct order.
   ● For instance, for a jam sandwich, this could be: 1. Spread the butter on both pieces of bread. 2. Spread the jam on one piece of bread. 3. Join the two pieces of bread. 4. Cut and serve.
   ● The children should then write out their instructions, adding drawings to explain each step.
   ● When this is done, ask them to make the food, following their instructions to check that they work.
   ● Eat and enjoy!

● Recipes and spells can offer an imaginative format for writing instructions. For instance, they could write:
   ● a spell for a story character – for instance, inspired by reading the *Meg and Mog* books by Helen Nicoll and Jan Pienkowski (Picture Puffin);
   ● a spell to make an angry teacher pie (a book full of scribbles, a class full of chatter…);
   ● a recipe for the best birthday party ever (1. Invite all your friends. 2. Open the huge pile of presents. 3. Eat a chocolate cake together…).

You Can... **Get creative with 'Ourselves'**

We all enjoy spending time thinking about, talking about and looking at ourselves. This applies particularly to young children, for whom the needs and concerns of others have relatively little importance. This topic can lend itself to some wonderfully creative and imaginative activities.

Thinking points

● There are plenty of cross-curricular links that can be made within this topic, in particular to work in art and science.

● Thinking about how we view ourselves, and the kind of image we present to the world, can help your children develop their social skills.

● This topic also gives the teacher scope for plenty of physical, hands-on activities which children seem to love.

Tips, ideas and activities

● Use body-related activities as a starter for this topic. You might try:
  ○ singing 'Heads, Shoulders, Knees and Toes';
  ○ playing *Simon Says*;
  ○ singing 'Dry Bones' (www.traditionalmusic.co.uk/childrens-songs/Dry_Bones(or_Skeleton_Bones).htm).

● Try this fun, physical exercise in an open space. It is a version of the popular game 'Twister':
  ○ Divide the class into pairs.
  ○ Say two body parts to the class (for example, hand, leg).
  ○ The children join these together, one part each (that is, one child's hand on the other's leg).
  ○ Say two more parts of the body (for example, nose, foot).
  ○ Keeping the first two parts connected, the children must join the second two parts together.
  ○ Keep going until everyone is completely twisted up!

● Use creative approaches to make some unusual self-portraits. Your children could use a mirror to:
  ○ draw an upside-down picture of themselves;
  ○ focus in on one part of their bodies (an eye, a finger), and draw an enlarged picture;
  ○ take 30 seconds to do a quick sketch of their own faces;
  ○ take photos of each other, cut these out and add them to a background drawing or a collage;
  ○ draw themselves in a costume that says something about them;
  ○ create a self-portrait using only lines, shapes or dots.

● Use the song 'My Favourite Things' from *The Sound of Music* to inspire some discussion work (see www.lyricsdownload.com/sound-of-music-my-favourite-things-lyrics.html). Ask children:
  ○ what the word 'favourite' means;
  ○ to write down their five favourite things;
  ○ to talk, in pairs, about why they like these things best;
  ○ to write down the five things they like least;
  ○ to talk, in pairs, about why they do not like these things.

You Can... Get creative with 'Homes'

Each of us has a home, whether it is a flat, a house or a palace, and for most of us, the idea of our 'home', helps us feel safe and rooted. Using stories and role play as a basis for exploring this theme will help you develop the children's creative thinking, about a topic which is close to their hearts.

Thinking points

● Homes are often a key feature for the characters in children's stories, and will typically have a symbolic meaning that goes deeper than a surface reading of the story. It is worth looking at these messages on a simple level with even the youngest pupils.

● When dealing with the theme of 'building', the teacher might find a tendency for the boys to take over, perhaps taking stereotypical attitudes about who 'does' construction. If this is the case with your class, make sure that you encourage the girls to get involved as well.

● This topic offers potential links right across the curriculum, and particularly to learning in history, geography and design and technology.

Tips, ideas and activities

● Use stories and songs to explore the theme of 'homes' in a creative way. Talk with the children about the messages of the different stories, and particularly what makes a 'good' home. For instance you may base talk on stories or songs such as:

● 'The Three Little Pigs' – build 'houses' from the different materials, using blocks instead of bricks, and then try blowing them down with a fan.

● 'The Wise Man and the Foolish Man' – as you sing, act out the building actions (see www.geocities.com/buildakid/songs/wise.html).

● 'Rapunzel' – get the children to build the tower where Rapunzel is trapped (for a version of the story, see www.storybookcastle.com/stories/stories/?source_file=rapunzel&pages=14&language=english).

● *Peepo!* by Janet and Allan Ahlberg (Viking Kestrel Picture Books) – talk about what homes were like in the past, spotting anything that would not be in a modern home.

● Set up a 'building site' in your role-play area, adding lots of construction costumes, props, etc. Encourage both boys and girls to get involved in role playing. You might include:

● a builder's hat;
● a high visibility jacket;
● some toy tools;
● blocks, play dough, clay and other materials for building;
● books related to building machines and processes;
● photos of builders at work;
● brochures about new build homes;
● photocopies of architectural plans.

● Use stories as an inspiration for looking at the kinds of homes where different animals live. For example:

● *The Very Hungry Caterpillar* by Eric Carle (Picture Puffin).
● *Aaaarrgghh, Spider!* by Lydia Monks (Egmont Books).
● *Sharing a Shell* by Julia Donaldson and Lydia Monks (Macmillan Children's Books).

● Use *The Jolly Postman* by Janet Ahlberg (Viking Kestrel Picture Books) to inspire discussion about the homes of different characters. Ask the children to write a postcard that their favourite story character might receive.

You Can... Get creative with 'Choices'

The idea that we can and should make the right choices, and that we must take responsibility for our actions, is an important lesson to learn. Many teachers now use this idea as a tool for managing behaviour – the idea that the child has a choice and, if he or she makes the wrong decision, that there are consequences that will be earned.

Thinking points
● Drama activities offer a great way to approach the theme of 'choices'. By taking on the parts of different characters, your pupils can learn about the viewpoints that people might have on a topic.

● In the past, people's behaviour was often supported by their religious beliefs. The teachings of different faiths helped children learn how to make good moral decisions. In an increasingly secular society, it is ever more important for children to think about the ethics of the choices they make.

● This theme has many cross-curricular links, particularly to citizenship, drama and religious education. It can also be used to encourage lots of thinking about moral and philosophical issues.

Tips, ideas and activities
● Try this drama activity called 'The Judgement Chair', to explore the choices that people make, and the impact that these choices have on others. Here is how it works:
  ● Think of a character who has made a bad choice, for instance, a child who has decided to become a bully.
  ● Ask for a volunteer to play the bully – this person sits in a chair known as 'The Judgement Chair'.
  ● Talk with the children about all the different people who might have an opinion about this person's behaviour. This might include: the victim, the victim's parents, the bully's parents, the child's teacher, the victim's friends.
  ● The pupils take it in turns to go up to the person in the Judgement Chair, and pass judgement on their behaviour.
  ● The victim might say, 'You made my life miserable, I'm scared to come into school'.
  ● The person in the Judgement Chair can respond (for example, defending the behaviour or apologising) or can stay silent instead.
  ● Talk about how it feels to be judged and whether this could change someone's behaviour.

● The paired drama exercises below look at how we might persuade someone to do something that they should not do, and ways of standing-up to pressure:
  ● 'Yes/No': One pupil says 'yes', the other says 'no'. Experiment with different ways of saying the words, for instance a 'no' that is like a 'yes'.
  ● 'Let's do it': pupils persuade their partners to do something wrong, such as stealing or lying. Afterwards, they should talk about the methods they used.
  ● 'Buy it': one pupil in each pair plays a salesperson trying to sell a pointless gadget to a customer – they improvise the scene.
  ● 'Excuse me': One child plays a pupil, the other a teacher. The pupil has not done his or her homework, and tries to persuade the teacher not to punish him or her.

You Can... Get creative with 'Health and growth'

Most teachers are all too aware of how important healthy food is for children – not only in terms of helping them grow, but also as an important factor in developing concentration and encouraging good behaviour.

Thinking points

● This topic lends itself to some wonderful sensory activities, particularly to the idea of smelling and tasting many different foods.

● While you might not be able to influence what foods children are given at home, you can certainly help your pupils to make informed decisions about what they do and do not want to eat.

● With healthy eating now firmly on the schools' agenda, now is the perfect time to inspire your children to try a wide range of good foods.

Tips, ideas and activities

● Use paper plates and modelling materials to create different kinds of meals. You might make models of:
  ● a healthy meal and an unhealthy one;
  ● a balanced meal;
  ● a meal for a special occasion.

● Make a block graph of your children's favourite foods, using a creative approach. You could:
  ● create a collage effect with packaging, sticking on sweet wrappers, crisp packets, etc.;
  ● cut out images from magazines to add to your graph;
  ● take digital photos of the different foods and add these to a graph created on the computer.

● Make a height chart by measuring each member of the class, and recording the information. Repeat at various points over the year, seeing how much your pupils grow.

● This character-based activity will encourage your children to think about healthy and unhealthy eating:
  ● Bring in two empty packed lunch boxes.
  ● Explain that one belongs to 'Healthy Harry'– the other to 'Junk Food Jenny'.
  ● Show a range of both processed foods (crisps, white bread sandwiches, lemonade, etc.) and healthier options (carrot sticks, brown bread sandwiches, water, etc.). Ask the children to sort the healthy foods into Harry's lunch box and the unhealthy ones into Jenny's.
  ● Explain to the pupils that Jenny is going to come into their classroom. Their aim is to get her to swap some of her junk food for some of Harry's healthy food.
  ● Say: *I'll just go and get her now*. Leave the room and put on a 'costume' (perhaps a cardigan or a coat). Come back 'in role' as Jenny.
  ● The children must get you to swap some of your food, telling you good things about the healthy foods, and vice versa, and perhaps using other, more creative approaches.

● See www.food.gov.uk/healthiereating/nutritionschools/ for more ideas to encourage healthy eating in schools.

You Can... Get creative with 'Labelling and classifying'

The concept that objects have particular characteristics, and that we can sort them according to these characteristics, is crucial for work in a variety of subject areas. You can introduce the children to a wide range of descriptive vocabulary during the course of this topic.

Thinking points

● While this has the potential to be a rather dull topic, by incorporating an active and creative backdrop to the work, the children will become fully engaged with what they are learning.

● Labelling and classifying can often be a fairly subjective exercise. In order to define what is 'big' or 'long', we might need to set some parameters beforehand.

● This ICT-based topic has many cross-curricular links, particularly to work in maths on shape and size, and to literacy work on description.

Tips, ideas and activities

● Try this drama activity to get your children thinking about how we describe different items:
  ● Place an interesting object in the classroom, such as a pen or a photograph.
  ● Enter the room as a forgetful elderly person, looking very concerned.
  ● Explain to the children that you have 'lost' something important, but you cannot remember its name.
  ● Describe the object to the pupils and ask them to work out what it is.
  ● They might ask you questions, as in the game 'Twenty Questions'.
  ● Get the children to locate the object for you.

● This fun, competitive activity asks the children to look for familiar objects that can be classified in a particular way:
  ● Divide the class into groups of four or six.
  ● Write a series of words that describe the characteristics of an object; for instance, long, big, small, red.
  ● Give on of these words, to the first group (for example 'long') and say: *Go.*
  ● Each group has one minute of thinking/talking time, and then 30 seconds to gather as many classroom objects, with this characteristic, as they can.
  ● The other groups could also glance around the room for any items that they would choose, while they are waiting their turn.
  ● Give the next group a different word (such as 'big') and say: *Go.*
  ● Repeat until all the groups have had a turn. Count the objects collected by each group to see who has won.
  ● Talk about how the children made their selection. Some characteristics should be easy for them to define (for example, 'red'), others may be more difficult (for example, 'big').

● Explore how we can write out words in a way that describes their characteristics. For instance, the word 'tiny' might be written as 'tiny', and the word 'long' as 'l o n g'.

You Can... **Get creative with 'Improving the environment'**

The idea of taking care of our environment, and of recycling and reusing our waste, is of course becoming ever more important. By starting close to home, and looking at the waste that we create in our homes and schools, you can help encourage the next generation to care for their world.

Thinking points

● This topic offers a great opportunity for bringing lots of props and objects into your classroom. Many of these objects are easily obtainable, but will add a real level of interest to the work. Let the children take a 'hands-on' approach wherever possible.

● This theme also provides lots of chances for the children to get out of the classroom and into the school and also the local area. Connecting the topic to their own environment will help engage them with the learning that takes place.

● This geography-based theme has cross-curricular links, particularly to learning in science, and also to using ICT to work with information.

Tips, ideas and activities

● Ask your children to work as 'government scientists' and to undertake a survey of the school environment. If possible, give the pupils white coats and clipboards to add a sense of realism to the project.

● Devise a school recycling slogan (for instance, based on the idea of 'Reduce, Reuse, Recycle'). Create posters to display around the school.

● To explore noise pollution in the school, get volunteers to wear a blindfold and stand in a position where there are high noise levels. Ask the pupils how it felt to be exposed to high levels of noise.

● With older (Year 3) children, bring in a bin bag of 'rubbish' and sort through it, wearing plastic gloves. You might include:
  ● cardboard and plastic packaging;
  ● various kinds of paper;
  ● empty plastic bottles;
  ● tinfoil;
  ● a (clean!) disposable nappy;
  ● old clothing and pairs of shoes;
  ● broken plastic children's toys;
  ● garden waste, such as twigs and leaves;
  ● some old books.

● As you look at the rubbish, ask the pupils to:
  ● identify which items might be reused or recycled;
  ● think about how the waste level can be reduced in some way (for example, by using cloth nappies);
  ● consider which items could be given to another person to reuse (for instance, via a charity shop);
  ● identify those items that are difficult to recycle, and consider how to overcome this (for instance, by buying wooden rather than plastic toys);
  ● look at how ICT can help us recycle (for example, reusing books via www.readitswapit.co.uk);
  ● establish which items could be recycled via a local council recycling scheme.

You Can... Get creative with 'Signs and symbols in religion'

Our world is filled with signs and symbols, not just in a religious context, but also in our day-to-day lives. Even at a young age, your children will be able to tell you what various visual signs and symbols 'mean'; understanding how imagery and symbolism can be created by language is a trickier concept for them to grasp.

Thinking points

● The concept that images can have both a literal and a symbolic meaning is a relatively high-level thinking skill. It is, however, possible for children to understand this idea, even from a fairly young age.

● Modern-day children are surrounded by signs and symbols, often in the context of different 'brands'. Many of them will already be very familiar with symbols related to food and consumer goods.

● This topic has a number of cross-curricular links, particularly to the creative writing and poetry strands in English. It also connects closely to the study of symbolism in art and design.

Tips, ideas and activities

● As a starting point for study of this topic, help your children complete the photocopiable sheet on page 61 ('Signs and symbols'). Ask the pupils to identify the symbols that they might find in different religions, and talk about what these signs might mean.

● Alternatively, show the class lots of objects in a specific colour (for instance, blue). Talk about how the colour makes us feel, and the kind of things it could symbolise. You might:
   ● wear some blue clothes;
   ● bring in some blue flowers;
   ● show images of blue flags;
   ● bring in photos of the sea, the sky, etc.

● Play the game of 'Dingbats' to help older (Year 3) children understand how words can have both literal and non-literal meanings. Here is how it works:
   ● Write out a series of common, non-literal sayings, choosing ones that are easy to translate into pictures.
   ● Some examples are: 'It's raining cats and dogs', 'Too hot to handle', 'Under the weather'.
   ● For more ideas, see www.youramazingbrain.org/teachers/dingbats.htm.
   ● Demonstrate how the game works – you will need a flipchart or several large sheets of paper.
   ● Draw one of the sayings; for instance, cats and dogs falling from a cloud.
   ● Challenge the pupils to guess what the saying is.
   ● Now ask for volunteers to have a go at drawing some sayings (younger children might need help with this).
   ● Afterwards, talk about what the sayings mean, and how we use them.

● Divide the class into small groups and ask them to produce a picture or collage for the religious sayings below. Talk about both their literal and non-literal meanings:
   ● 'God is my rock' (Psalms 18: 2);
   ● 'Wealth maketh many friends' (Proverbs 19: 4);
   ● 'Jesus is the light of the world' (John 18: 12).

You Can... Get creative with 'Puppets'

Children are often fascinated by puppets – there is something magical about seeing an inanimate object being 'brought to life' by the person operating it. There are many different kinds of puppet you might create – from the simple finger or sock puppet, to the more complex marionette.

Thinking points

- As well as thinking about the moods and emotions that the puppets will have, get your children to think about how they might speak or the kind of noises they would make.

- This design and technology theme has obvious links to drama and storytelling. Music might also be incorporated into a puppet show.

- In addition, you could look at the history of puppets. Look at www.lepetitprince.com/en/ROI/histoire_marionnette.php for a brief outline.

Tips, ideas and activities

- Try this drama exercise as an active starter for this theme:
  - Work in an open space, with the children, in pairs.
  - One child in each pair is the 'puppet' and the other is the 'puppet master'.
  - The puppet has invisible strings at various points on his or her body.
  - To start with, these are on the head, hands, elbows, knees and feet.
  - As the puppet master 'pulls' the string, the puppet moves that part of the body.
  - The aim is to make it look as though there are actually strings attached.
  - Get half of the class to watch the other half moving their puppets – talk about who is doing it well and why.
  - As the pupils get more confident, make their puppets interact (for instance, shaking hands). Add more strings (for instance, on the fingers).

- Scholastic has published books incorporating finger and hand puppets, which would be great for this theme – see www.scholastic.co.uk/zone/book_hand-puppets.htm for details. See also *The Muppets Make Puppets* by Cheryl Henson (Workman Publishing).

- Take this topic one stage further, by getting the children to make their own theatre, and perform some of their puppet shows to an audience. To make a theatre:
  - Get hold of a large cardboard box – one big enough for the children to stand inside.
  - Create a square flap, cutting around the top and the two sides. The flap can be folded up and down as a 'curtain'.
  - Decorate the box with paint or a collage effect.
  - Choose a name for your puppet theatre.
  - Design some backdrops – position these on the back wall of the box, so that they are seen behind the puppets.
  - Devise and present your shows!

You Can... Get creative with 'Feel the pulse'

This is a lovely theme, and there is plenty of scope within it for creative activity, particularly that which connects movement, dance and drama. The idea that we have a pulse but can also feel a pulse in music, leads to some interesting creative connections.

Thinking points

● Hearing a strong, regular beat gives us an almost irresistible urge to move. There are links here to the heartbeat that we hear in the womb – a rhythm that stays with us as we grow up and gives us a sense of security.

● This topic allows you to introduce the idea that language, particularly poetic language, has a rhythm inherent within it.

● Although this theme is music-based, it clearly has links to other subject areas such as science or dance in PE.

Tips, ideas and activities

● Do some activities based around the idea of taking a pulse:
  ● Get your children to take their pulses, by placing the three middle fingers of their right hands on the inside wrist of their left hand.
  ● Here is a useful web page with a description and some visual resources: www.galaxy-h.gov.uk/your-body-and-activity04.html.
  ● Ask your children to think about why they should not use a thumb to take their pulses.
  ● Try taking a pulse measurement before and after some exercise.

● Take the class into an open space for some movement activities based around the idea of pulse. Here are two ideas:
  ● Get the children walking around the space to the regular beat of a drum. Gradually speed the drumbeat up and then slow it down. Afterwards, talk about how the different speeds felt.
  ● Use the game 'Leader of the Band' – a volunteer leaves the room while a 'leader' is chosen. This person leads the class in a series of rhythmic activities, such as clapping a rhythm and then banging it with hands, on the floor. The volunteer must work out who the 'leader' is.

● Use the photocopiable sheet on page 62 ('Macbeth') to look at rhythm and pulse in language:
  ● Read the scene several times. Ask the children to identify any vocabulary they do not understand, and discuss what these words mean.
  ● Read the scene again, this time with the pupils adding a rhythmic pulse. Use eight beats in four double taps. Put emphasis on the second beat of each pair. Say the first word 'when' on the second beat.
  ● Dramatise the scene by dividing the class into four groups. Give three of the groups the words of one of the witches each, and the fourth group the job of adding atmospheric sound effects.

You Can... Get creative with 'Toys from the past'

Toys are a great way of encouraging creative play – a simple pile of wooden blocks can lead to a myriad of activities, from tower building to counting. Many toys also have a clear element of character, and children will often use them to experiment with building stories.

Thinking points

● Modern children tend to have a lot of toys, but sometimes it seems that these toys are less well taken care of than in the past.

● You might have noticed that children will actually play much more creatively with very simple, often natural materials, such as mud, water, twigs, leaves and sand.

● The idea of toys, of course, goes back for many thousands of years. Figuring out how primitive toys might have been made and used can lead to some very creative thinking.

● This history theme has links with subject areas such as design and technology. There is also the potential for a lot of literacy work.

Tips, ideas and activities

● Rather than giving the children adjectives to match to different toys, why not create a matching game with the children yourself?

  ○ As a class, brainstorm all the descriptive words we might apply to toys from the present and the past.
  ○ Write the best suggestions on a set of small cards and put the cards in a bag.
  ○ Now get the children to stand in a circle, with a pile of old and new toys in the middle.
  ○ Hand the bag around. Each child must dip into the bag and pull out an adjective, then run into the middle and pick up a toy that matches the word.
  ○ You might challenge the class to beat a set time, to get them really engaged and thinking quickly.

● Look on the web for more ideas about toys in the past. There is a useful (if brief) timeline of toy history at www.history.com/exhibits/toys/timeline.html and a brief history of toys at www.hants.gov.uk/museum/toys/history/.

● Take the idea of making a 'toy museum' into your classroom, and spice it up a bit. You could:

  ○ get the children to pose in tableaux as 'animatronic' toys. When the visitor (you) presses a button, the toys come to life, perform a short scene, and then freeze again;
  ○ use the idea of a closed-down and deserted toy museum. Ask some of the pupils to pose as haunted toys, and some to sneak into the museum, holding torches. As the pupils look around, they talk about what they see, creating a sense of atmosphere. Some of the toys come to life and play tricks on them;
  ○ set up a scenario at the toy museum; for instance, that a valuable toy has been stolen. Get the children to look for evidence, interview witnesses, devise a theory and so on.

What's my animal?

Discussion:
- Imagine each animal is a person. What would that person be like?

Activity:
- Match the words to each animal.

Thinking:
- Which animal are you like when you work in a group?
- Can you be like a different animal next time you work in a group?

wise	hardworking	strong	loud	patient	watchful
shy	busy	quiet	brave	gentle	talkative
listens	lively	leads	thoughtful		

Creative thinking

The book is called: ....

The author is: ....

The character who has a problem is: ....

Draw a picture of the problem:

How does the character solve the problem?

....

....

Think of some other ways to solve the problem. Draw one of your ideas here:

The weather

- Write sentences about the weather.
- Draw a picture to go with each kind of weather.

I am the sun

I am ....

I feel..

I am the rain

I am ....

I feel..

I sound..

I am the snow

I am..

I feel..

I am the wind

I feel..

I sound..

The birthday cake

Design a birthday cake for your favourite story character!

My favourite story character is:...

Draw your character in the space below:

Decorate your birthday cake here:

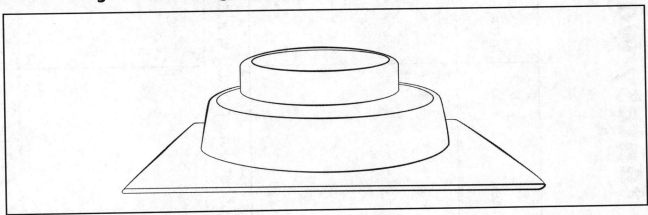

Now write some instructions for decorating your cake:

You will need: ....

....

1. ....

2. ....

3. ....

4. ....

Wordbank: add, cut, put, roll, spread, sprinkle, stick, icing, cherries, chocolate, cream, coconut, candles, flakes, ribbon, strawberries, sweets

My fantasy world

My fantasy world is ....

See	Hear	Smell	Taste	Touch

Now draw a cartoon strip or plan a story about your fantasy world.

Signs and symbols

- Look at the symbols and talk about what they mean.
- Write the words in under the correct pictures.
- Which of these symbols are found in religion? Draw a circle around them.

....	....
....	....
....	....
....	....
....	....
....	....

candle	rainbow	dove	khanda	tick	cross
menorah	Star of David	star and crescent	arrow	yin and yang	fish

You Can... **Have a creative classroom 4–7**

Macbeth

Act 1, Scene 1

Thunder and lightning. Enter three witches.

First witch:
When shall we three meet again
In thunder, lightning, or in rain?

Second witch:
When the hurlyburly's done,
When the battle's lost and won.

Third witch:
That will be ere the set of sun.

First witch:
Where the place?

Second witch:
Upon the heath.

Third witch:
There to meet with Macbeth.

First witch:
I come, Graymalkin!

Second witch:
Paddock calls.

Third witch:
Anon.

All:
Fair is foul, and foul is fair:
Hover through the fog and filthy air.

Index

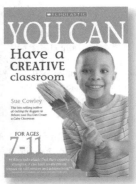